ORACLES *of* GRACE

Building a Legacy of Wisdom and Revelation

WANDA ALGER

Alger Publications
Winchester, VA

Oracles of Grace: Building a Legacy of Wisdom and Revelation
by Wanda Alger

Published by
Alger Publications
Winchester, VA
wandaalger.me

ISBN-13: 978-0999675205
ISBN-10: 0999675206

Cover art and photographs by Rachel Alger

Cover photograph by Greg Rakozy

ENDORSEMENTS

"Her pen shakes the heavens and the earth, and rattles the gates of hell. I am honored to know the one who holds that pen, Wanda Alger, and the One who holds her close to His heart."

– **BILL YOUNT**, speaker; author, *The Power of Real*

"Quality writing impresses me. But quality writing about walking in God's grace impresses me a lot! This is a book to take you from where you are, in a straight line to where you want to be…to where you *need* to be. *Oracles of Grace* is a book that draws you softly and carefully into that grace without the trappings of legalism. You need to get this book."

– **STEVE SCHULTZ**, Publisher, The Elijah List

"Are you ready to fall into our Father's heart through a passionate pursuit with greater power and results? I highly recommend this book to bring you into alignment with His heart and what He is doing on this earth. The scriptures that Wanda uses create a solid foundation to the powerful revelation and life-giving applications that she unfolds.

– **DALE L. MAST**, Senior Pastor, Destiny Church, Dover, Delaware; author, *And David Perceived He Was King*

"I love Wanda's new book, *Oracles of Grace*! This book is filled with divine wisdom and revelation and encourages each of us to fulfill our God-given destiny. She shares of God's redeeming grace discovered during great pain, as well as from times of great joy.

— **LAVERNE KREIDER**, co-founder and apostolic leader, DOVE International

"*Oracles of Grace* comes from the depths of real life providing tangible insights. It will guide any wise reader to places of intimacy with God. Wanda's heart was touched by God and she will touch yours."

– **DAVID KUBAL**, President, Intercessors for America

"Read this book! The best books written are by authors who walk the walk and talk the talk. Such a writer is Wanda Alger. I can personally attest that *Oracles of Grace* was penned by one who knows the secret place from firsthand experience. Her anointed words will draw your heart closer to the Lord. Whether a novice or grizzled warrior, *Oracles of Grace* has the potential for life-changing breakthroughs with Him!

– **BRIAN FRANCIS HUME**, National Prayer Director, Awaken the Dawn

"I recommend this book very highly to those who wish to break free from the unending complexities and challenges of these times, to simply knowing Him, and living out His grace in our lives. This call to authentic Christianity rings loud and clear throughout the pages of *Oracles of Grace*.

– **SARA BALLENGER**, Founder and president, Capitol Hill Prayer Partners

"They say the most important meal of the day is breakfast. Wanda does an excellent job providing a spiritual breakfast for starting each day. You will be encouraged, enlightened, and challenged as she provides short insights into many of the things that you most likely missed in the past. It is truly a spiritual breakfast for champions."

– **RON MYER**, Assistant International Director, DOVE International

"Chock full of wisdom that can only come from a life of obedience, *Oracles of Grace* is an invitation to life in the Kingdom. I wholeheartedly recommend it."

– **BRANDON SHOWALTER**, journalist

To the ones whom I carry in my heart with great affection and love:

Rachel Elizabeth *– My firstborn who carries a double portion of gifting from your father and me. Your creative expression and adventurous spirit have taught me to see the joy in the journey. You are a shining example of what a daughter of the King is supposed to look like.*

Nathaniel Robert (Nate) *– My firstborn son who carries a deep well of revelation and spiritual hunger. Your passion for truth and pursuit of eternal things touches my heart with great joy. You are a fiery trailblazer who is making a way for others to reach the stars.*

Joshua Joel (Josh) *– I knew when you were young that you would go places and pioneer things that few ever dream of. For you, nothing will ever be impossible. Your life and testimony continue to overwhelm me with gratitude as to the endless potential in store for those who believe.*

"ORACLE"
"a brief utterance of God, declaration, revelation"
(Strong's Exhaustive Concordance)

As each has received a gift, use it to serve one another, as good
stewards of God's varied grace: whoever speaks,
as one who speaks oracles of God.
1 Peter 4:10

For though by this time you ought to be teachers, you need someone
to teach you again the basic principles of the oracles of God.
Hebrews 5:12

CONTENTS

INTRODUCTION

For years growing up, I would spend a lot of time in my room playing my guitar, reading, and journaling. This wasn't necessarily because I was a deeply spiritual person. It was because it was the only place I could go where I felt safe and secure. Being a pastor's kid may have given me the benefit of growing up in the church, but there was a dark underside.

My father grew up in an orphanage with his two siblings and never got over his feelings of rejection, pain, and anger. Though he sincerely loved God and knew he was called as an evangelist, the demons from his past surfaced at home. At church, his outward behavior demonstrated affirmation, generosity, and an abundance of good works, but at home the outbursts of criticism, outrage, and disapproval became toxic to me and my siblings and there was constant tension. One never knew when Dad might come home and raise his voice, and sometimes his fist, against one of his own who didn't comply with his expectations. My siblings and I would react differently, but each one of us was marked by the unresolved restlessness and rejection that my father carried with him during those early years.

By God's grace and mercy, it was in these years that my call to the secret place was born. It was my hidden place where I could be alone with God, uninterrupted by the chaos outside. Being a shy introvert who loved music and the arts, I found my solace in the privacy of my bedroom. The Living Bible Paraphrase had just been published and it became my life-line at a time when I felt trapped and helpless to change anything. I started a journal of verses that I could pray in hopes that, somehow, things might eventually get better.

Throughout my high school years, I saw little tangible evidence that God was doing anything to change things at home. My times with Him were more a place of comfort and security than a source of true power and answered prayer. Perhaps I didn't really expect Him to do anything other than just help me get through it. Even so, a daily routine became embedded in my life and I never turned back.

Establishing this secret place became foundational for the years that followed. Regardless of what happened, I knew there was a place I could go for assurance and hope.

You are a hiding place for me; You preserve me from trouble;
You surround me with shouts of deliverance.
Psalm 32:7

As I look back over those years and even the journals I wrote, I am struck by God's grace. Even then God's Spirit was at work in me, giving me wisdom and revelation as to what was happening in my life. Many of the verses I underlined in my Bible at that time focused my attention, not on what was seen, but what was unseen (2 Corinthians 4:18). I learned to grow in my discernment of what the Spirit was saying, regardless of what my own head or other voices said. Where the enemy tried to sow discouragement and despair, the Lord was sowing truth and wisdom that fueled my prayers. Even during the darkest times, He was nurturing my faith to trust in His heart to take care of things I never could.

When I eventually experienced the baptism of the Holy Spirit in my early twenties, my secret place transformed from a place of safety and security, to a place of empowered prayer and declaration. I became emboldened in my faith and began to see things happen as I declared God's heart and purpose in my life and the lives of those around me. Even in my own family, I began to see prayers answered that were spoken years earlier. His Word was not only the source of truth for me, it became a living, active agent that enabled me to partner with the Father in bringing heaven to earth. Prayer is not merely an exercise or religious duty, but a place of intimate fellowship and powerful transaction with the Father. When we practice His presence on a consistent basis, our daily walk becomes a never-ending prayer to Him. Thus, we are all joining with Jesus as our Great Intercessor before the Father.

Consequently, He is able to save to the uttermost those
who draw near to God through Him, since
He always lives to make intercession for them.
Hebrews 7:25

We have daily opportunities to change things for the better and to see lives transformed. We can only do this when we have established a daily time with the Lord and walk from the place of His presence. Otherwise, we will be running on our own steam and will soon burn out. It's not so much the amount of time you spend, as much as the consistency and routine. If we truly want to know Him, it will come from a daily awareness of His presence and hearing His voice.

This book is a tool I hope can equip and empower you to establish a secret place in your own life. The truths that have become foundational in my own life are written throughout. It is my prayer that His truth and the power of His Spirit will speak to your heart through the "oracles" God has given me so that you can be a conduit of heaven right where you are.

At the end of each entry is a prayer based on Scriptures mentioned. I believe the best way to get God's Word into our lives is to pray it. I encourage you to look up each Scripture that is listed and use it as a prayer in your own life. Take notes and keep track of how God responds to you, because He will! He has so much to show you and so much to tell you.

I do not cease to give thanks for you, remembering you in my prayers, that the God of our Lord Jesus Christ, the Father of glory, may give you the Spirit of wisdom and of revelation in the knowledge of Him, having the eyes of your hearts enlightened, that you may know what is the hope to which He has called you, what are the riches of His glorious inheritance in the saints, and what is the immeasurable greatness of His power toward us who believe. Ephesians 1:16-19.

An Invitation *to the* Secret Place

Yet among the mature we do impart wisdom, although it is not a wisdom of this age or of the rulers of this age, who are doomed to pass away. But we impart a secret and hidden wisdom of God, which God decreed before the ages for our glory.

1 Corinthians 2:6-7

IT'S ALL ABOUT PERSPECTIVE

Why do we even come to the secret place with the Lord? What draws us there in the first place? Is it a need? A desire? A problem to be solved? What compels us to take the time to be with Someone we can't even see or talk with face to face?

Human nature is always looking for shortcuts. We want a quick fix to our problems and we want someone else to do the work. It isn't easy to wait for answers. The idea of taking the time to watch, listen, and pray can be frustrating to those who need help. Now!

Yet, if we really saw what God sees, it would totally change our motivation for why we come to Him in the first place. Most of us are preoccupied about ourselves and our own problems along with the need to fix things. In our efforts to put out the fires of today, we don't have the time or emotional bandwidth to consider the possibilities of tomorrow.

Call to Me and I will answer you and tell you great and unsearchable things you do not know.
Jeremiah 33:3

It's all about perspective.

I believe God has things in store for us that are so unimaginable and amazing that there is no way our human thinking can comprehend them. This is why He will use the struggles, setbacks, and problems in our lives to *compel* us to come to Him. He'll do whatever it takes to get our attention because He's eager to share His secrets with us. He is continually calling out our names in hopes that we will hear His voice and respond.

Yet, in His calling out, He seems to play hide-and-seek with us. Just as He spoke to His followers in parables, so He often speaks to us, today. Rather than handing us our future on a silver platter, He calls us into the secret place to journey with Him. He purposely avoids giving us all the answers we are looking for because, ultimately, He wants us to seek HIM.

It's about the journey.

He is looking for His sons and daughters to take His hand and simply walk with Him. The secret place is a place of adventure. It is about discovery, revelation, and destiny. It is a place to consider the possibilities, even in our pain. It is the place where dreams can come true and mysteries can be solved. Yes, He will help us put out the daily fires we face, but even more, He longs to show us the incredible possibilities of tomorrow. It depends on our hunger and our desire for *more*.

What is your expectation? Do you limit your secret place to just fixing problems or do you linger, considering His dreams for you and the unknown opportunities ahead? He is not just a loving Father that can give you good counsel. He is the Pioneer and Trail Blazer. He is the Champion of all who seek greater things for He loves the adventure.

Determine to come into the secret place expecting to see things you've never seen before, hear things you've never heard before, and understand things you've never understood before. He's waiting.

Heavenly Father, I thank You for the invitation to the secret place. I am calling out to You, now. Stir in me an even greater desire to not only know Your heart, but to know the great and unsearchable things that You have for me. Increase my faith so that I might embrace and understand all that You show me. Increase my hunger so that I will consistently draw closer to You with great expectation of our walk together. Teach me how to establish this sacred time and sacred place with You so that my life will be full and complete in You. Thank you for the amazing times ahead. In Jesus' name, amen!

ETERNITY IS IN YOUR HEART

He has made everything beautiful in its time.
He has also set eternity in the human heart; yet no one can
fathom what God has done from beginning to end.
Ecclesiastes 3:11

Scripture tells us that this life is very brief (James 4:14) and our troubles are very momentary (2 Corinthians 4:17). Yet, when we are in the midst of challenging situations with big questions looming before us, it's hard to think of life outside of our current circumstances.

The Word says God has put eternity in our hearts. The word "eternity" means "always, continuous existence, perpetual, everlasting, indefinite, or unending future." It means that whatever is going to last, whatever is going to perpetuate for all time, whatever truly matters in life, *that* is what He has given us the potential to live *from* and to live *for*. A deposit has already been placed in our heart for everything that is real, true, and forever! And, it's up to us to discover it.

I want my life to matter. I want to make a difference. A BIG difference! I don't want to waste my time only to look back as I stand before my Creator on that Last Day and see that I missed out on His plans, purposes, and promises *simply because I had no imagination for it*. I have determined to believe that if He has placed possibilities within me, then He's given me the grace to discover those possibilities and walk them out (2 Corinthians 9:8). Not only does this promise give me hope for my future, it gives me the proper perspective of my place in eternity. It reminds me that there is another reality that I live in and live from.

1 Chronicles 29:15 states we are "…foreigners and strangers" and that "…our days on earth are like a shadow." Colossians 3:2 reminds us to "…set your minds on things that are above, not on things that are on earth." Philippians 3:20 states "…our citizenship is in heaven."

With eternity in my heart, I live with the daily reality that I come from another place. I was born of the earth, but also born of the Spirit (Genesis 2:7). I am created from a supernatural realm that is far greater and more powerful than this earthly realm. I am seated with Christ in heavenly places because that's where I came from (Psalm 139:13)!

If we but realized the very essence of our DNA and the miraculous potential we live with, we wouldn't waste another minute. We are not limited to our abilities, talents, and skill sets. We are not determined by what others say about us or by the surroundings of our life. We do not have to be hindered or held back just because we don't see with our natural eyes or hear with our natural ears what God is doing in us and through us (1 Corinthians 2:9-10).

We were created from an eternal substance that is alive and active within our hearts.

Jesus said that we would do greater things than He did, precisely because of this reality, and He gave us access through the cross. Now, "eternity" is waiting for us to live like it!

Are you aware of eternity within your own heart? Do you wake up with the knowledge that you have the same power within you that raised Christ from the dead? Are you living each day with the possibility of miracles in and through your life?

Thank You, Heavenly Father, for placing eternity within my heart. Thank You for the endless possibilities that lie before me. Open my eyes that I might see what You see, to hear what You hear, and to know what You know. May I live from the reality of Your Spirit which brings abundant life, miraculous victories, and endless discoveries. Give me the childlike wonder of the heavenly realms so that I might use my time on the earth to help others see how amazing You are and how loved they are. In Jesus's name, amen.

ARE YOU WILLING TO GET UNCOMFORTABLE?

As I was praying about my own level of spiritual hunger one day, I had to admit my challenge in consistently looking for Him. It's my natural tendency to look at the *last place* I "found" Him. I want something that's familiar – it simply makes it easier. Sometimes, I just get tired of looking for Him. One day I declared my desire to seek His heart and cried out, "Lord, where ARE You!?"

He simply smiled and said, "In Unfamiliar Places. Come, find Me!"

That which many of us seek will only be found in Unfamiliar Places. He is encouraging us to step out in faith and be willing to get uncomfortable. That's where He is – the unfamiliar places in our own lives that will cause us to see Him like we've never seen Him before, and to know Him in ways we have not known Him before.

You won't have to look for those places. God will invite you there Himself and open the door. He will present you with opportunities to do something new – to try something you haven't done before. It will, most likely, even be something you are uncomfortable with. It will require new levels of faith and trust. However, your level of comfort is not the determining factor – it's your faith and your hunger to know Him that will compel you to respond.

Abraham was invited to Unfamiliar Places (Genesis 12:1). He didn't hesitate – he just went. His hunger to know his God outweighed that which was familiar to him. He was willing to leave everything he knew in order to satisfy the longing within his spirit for something "more" (Hebrews 11:10).

This is not just an exercise of faith, but a matter of spiritual hunger.

If our focus is truly on *knowing Him*, our desperate longing can fuel our passion and ignite our steps. His invitation is always there. We just have to get past our inhibitions and start the journey.

Look for Him in the Unfamiliar Places of your life. Let courage rise and faith be stirred. He is passionate about revealing Himself and is eagerly waiting for us to step over the threshold of the unknown. New levels of faith will be attained once we take that step. Grace which has never been accessed will now become available. New expressions and revelations will be found in these unfamiliar places. Instead of waiting to feel ready, it is in taking those steps that you shall *be made ready* and receive an upgrade and overflow of what your heart has been longing for.

Both personally and corporately, as we look for this "new thing" that God is about to do, we must step out of the boat, jump off the cliff, and come out of the cave. It is our faith in God and our desperate desire that will cause heaven to respond. We should not be waiting for Him, for He is waiting on us.

Pray for a greater spiritual hunger and desperation to arise in your heart and fuel your journey. It's okay to feel uncomfortable. It's an indicator that His Spirit has already begun to draw you. Accept His invitation, follow His lead, and don't look back. The true adventure is only just beginning!

*Forget the former things; do not dwell on the past. See, I am doing
a new thing! Now it springs up; do you not perceive it? I am
making a way in the wilderness and streams in the wasteland.*
Isaiah 43:18

Lord, I want to find You and am willing to get uncomfortable. Draw me into the new places You have for me. Give me the joy of the call that will outweigh any cost. Increase my faith to believe that You have great things in store for me in these hidden places. I lay down my own expectations and trade them in for Your promise to prosper me, to give me a hope and a future that is secure in You (Jeremiah 29:11). Thank You for the journey ahead! In Jesus' name, amen.

Relationship First

If we only pray to God for answers, revelations, or plans, we're missing His heart. His first priority with us is relationship. It's this relationship - this friendship - that opens the door to genuine encounter with Him and results in answered prayer.

Thus, the Lord used to speak to Moses face to face,
as a man speaks to his friend.
Exodus 33:11

God wants to *know* us and *be known*. That is the essence of true friendship and intimacy. Scripture says that God is jealous for us, (Deuteronomy 4:24) which means "to desire, to pursue with love, to long after." He is not only jealous for us, but zealous in taking down every spiritual enemy that comes against us (Isaiah 42:13).

We usually don't question God's *ability* to take care of us, but we often doubt His *desire* to.

We must be convinced of His redemptive purpose and compassionate commitment to us. As we spend time seeking His heart through His Word, our trust in Him grows, and our prayers will change. We will no longer pray out of fear or anxiety but out of confidence and rest (James 4:3-5, 1 John 5:15).

Some of us may have to work at this relationship aspect a bit more than others. My primary love language is doing acts of service. I am a high achiever who loves projects, creating new things, and getting things done. I've had to learn how to be still and just…chill.

God has never failed to meet me in the secret place and, many times, has surprised me with unexpected insights and ideas that came straight from His heart to mine. He knows how I'm wired and is just as excited about "doing things" as I am. He simply wants to be a part of the process.

For we are God's handiwork, created in Christ Jesus to do good works, which God prepared in advance for us to do.
Ephesians 2:10

As you establish the secret place in your life, know that He is not only aware of what stirs you the most; He created you that way and looks forward to walking with you in your journey of discovery.

Heavenly Father, I desire to truly know You and Your heart for me. I purpose to be real and vulnerable with You. Forgive my doubts about Your intentions for me and help me to grow in my faith as I study and stand on Your Word. Remind me throughout the day of Your presence and Your purposes for me. Reveal to me any areas that I am holding back from You. Draw me closer to Your heart and I will give You the praise and honor for the work You are accomplishing in and through my life. In Jesus' name, amen.

A Lover That's Bound
to No Other

It appears that God is fairly passionate about *unity* and *intimacy* being entwined. It was during a time of struggling in my own marriage that the Lord seemed to illustrate His heart for His Bride.

Though our marriage has always been solid and our covenant uncompromising, there was a season that lacked true intimacy. We had known it, but didn't know how to get past it. Our differences in personality and gifting had been a constant challenge both at home and in the ministry. The strongholds became glaring and I began to feel overwhelmed that things would never change. I didn't know if we would ever truly *connect*.

The Holy Spirit was revealing things that were holding our hearts captive – faulty mindsets, ungodly beliefs, inner wounds, and spiritual blindness to our true identities in Christ. I felt like we were being pulled from other directions and other people, bound to the responsibilities and obligations that were so familiar to us. We had no satisfaction or peace of mind. I knew that no gift, no level of anointing, and no amount of ministry experience was going to "fix" this. It was only an infilling of Perfect Love that would heal our hearts and set us free to truly know one another and Him.

I went to the Lord in prayer one day and began to cry out to Him regarding this issue. I knew I needed to lay everything down and get rid of the many obstacles that were keeping me from connecting to my husband and God. As I confessed the things that I was holding on to, I began to sense His presence.

My prayer and His voice began to sound as one. Even as I was praying my own heart, I began to feel as if I was praying His. I heard myself say, "I want a lover that's bound to no other!" I said it over and over and each time I did, I realized it was not just my cry, but His. I was feeling the passion, the longing, the desire of the Lord Jesus who was calling out to His sons and daughters, "I want a lover that's bound to no other!"

I realized that this was the key to freedom. I had been bound by so many other distractions and preoccupations that I was unable to truly bind myself to the Lord. These other things that I "loved" had become roadblocks to intimacy. My heart had been taken up with so many other "lovers" I was unable to connect to the Lover of my soul, or the lover I was married to.

As I released all these obstacles in my heart, His peace came. I felt a connection I'd been missing. I felt *bound* to Him, not just in my head, but in my heart. This oneness of heart enabled me to clear the way for a breakthrough with my husband and we were able to connect again in a much deeper way.

The Lord urgently desires to be the Lover of our souls, but we have been bound up by other things. Ministry responsibilities, friends, preoccupation with family or career, busyness, addictions, and other emotional crutches have taken our time and attention as we have sought to heal ourselves. In our need for affirmation and validation, we have sought to fill our hearts with lesser things and have thus bound ourselves to idols. There has been no room left for Him.

This is what the LORD Almighty says: "I am very jealous for Zion;
I am burning with jealousy for her."
Zechariah 8:2

We may have a sincere desire to draw close to the Lord. However, if we are distracted or preoccupied with other things, other priorities, and other relationships, we won't have any room left for Him. We may not realize how close we are to idolatry until we begin to start laying things down on the altar.

But seek first the kingdom of God and His righteousness, and all these things will be added to you.
Matthew 6:33

I urge you to search your heart to make sure there are no other lovers getting in the way of your relationship with Christ. Allow the Holy Spirit to reveal any hidden preoccupation or longing that is stronger than your desire for the Lord. Make His heart-cry your own and pray that you would be His lover, bound to no other.

I come to You, Lord Jesus, with the desire to be bound to Your heart above all others. I know that it is only in my intimacy with You that I can truly connect and give freely to others. Show me any idol or preoccupation in my life that is taking the place of You. Cleanse my heart and mind of any counterfeit and purify my longing for You. Bring me to true intimacy with You and the joy of loving fully and freely. May I overflow with this love to my family and friends so that they, too, may come to know the power of oneness with You. In Jesus' name, amen.

THE DIFFERENCE BETWEEN BELIEVERS AND LOVERS

The Father is looking for Lovers, not just Believers. While belief is the starting place for the journey to His heart, it must eventually lead to an intimacy that only Lovers can know.

There's a difference between a BELIEVER and a LOVER.

- A Believer thinks from his head; a Lover feels from his heart.

- A Believer clings to the written Word; a Lover clings to the Living Word.

- A Believer sees only what is; a Lover dreams of the possibilities.

- A Believer holds onto promises; a Lover holds onto Jesus.

- A Believer bravely stands in the trials; a Lover silently waits in His presence.

- A Believer works hard to keep the faith; a Lover simply rests in His embrace.

To be a Lover is to be abandoned and free, captivated by One, while a Believer struggles to keep the pace with distractions all around.

While belief is what tells us we can stand before a Holy God, it is Love that draws us beyond the throne and into the chambers of His heart. Belief is no longer the measure of our value, for we have been consumed by the One in Whom we believe.

Instead of looking at Him, we are now living from Him...He in us and us in Him. We have become one; fused together, bound, and interwoven so completely that we live and breathe as one.

Belief is the starting point in this journey, but Perfect Love replaces faith with the reality of a union so powerful, so complete, and so eternal that faith is no longer needed.

We just...are. And now, all things are possible.

THE CHAMBERS
OF HIS HEART

"I want to know your heart, God!" That was my cry. It had been the longing of my soul to truly know His heart.

I see Him motion for me to come. He points to His heart and invites me to come in. His heart opens up to reveal a huge chamber that beckons me to come - so I jump in!

This chamber of Love is beating, and the walls of His heart reverberate with every beat. As I stand in the center of His heart, the strength of each beat knocks me down. Unprepared for the strength of His heartbeat, I am caught unawares and repeatedly knocked to the ground with every beat. Beat after beat, I am struck and moved about in the chamber of His heart as this immense heart of Love is beating for His creation, longing for healing, salvation, and deliverance.

I was feeling the pain and depth of love for the bruised, the broken, the tormented ones. I said, "Lord, how am I to stand in this place? How am I to bear up under the intensity of Your heartbeat?"

He said, "My child, you wanted to know My heart, and this is the force of My love. I feel the pain and the wounding of My creation and My heart carries the burdens of those who are being destroyed by the enemy of their souls. To know My heart is to know the suffering of others and to carry these burdens with Me."

As I realized that this force of Love would not stop, I realized I needed to adjust and begin to move with His heartbeat and not fight against it. Rather than trying to protect myself, I chose to move with these pulsating beats, anticipating His moves and becoming one with Him. The heartbeat grew stronger and I was learning to stand even while taking the force of each beat.

This encounter changed my perspective on "wanting to know God's heart!" He allowed me to feel what He carries for each and every one of His creation. I realized the intensity of His love, the depth of His passion, and the intensity of His zeal in watching over and bringing freedom to His sons and daughters.

I was humbled and enlarged. Not only had I experienced just a bit of what He actually feels about me, but was challenged by the limitations of my love for others.

At first, I wasn't able to stand in the midst of this powerful Love. I had only been thinking of myself and what I was experiencing. I had to adjust my own heartbeat to His. There is a rhythm of His love and it is passionate and powerful. It requires me to get out of my own head and become one with His heart. It requires me to let go of self-preservation in order to move with Him. It requires me to give Him access to my own passions and desires so He can deposit Himself in their place.

If we truly want to "know His heart," we must be ready for it. Not only will we have access to His love for us, but we will become conduits of that love towards others.

It is His desire that we love others, not out of our own ability, feeling, or capacity, but from His heart.

When we can love others with the same love that He has, then there is no room for failure. Rather than trying to love someone else with our own hopes and expectations, we can love from this deep place of Unfailing Love. It is this place where we are free from offense, hurt, and fear because we are not loving from our own limited place, but from the chambers of His heart.

So, we have come to know and to believe the love that God has for us. God is love, and whoever abides in love abides in God, and God abides in him. By this is love perfected.
1 John 4:16-17a

Thank You for Your zealous and extravagant love for me, Father. I want to live from the chambers of Your heart and know Your heartbeat so that I can love others well. I determine to live from this place of Unfailing Love for You are worthy, Jesus! Amen.

GETTING A
HEART TRANSPLANT

Loving people isn't easy. Maybe for some people it's easier than others, but all of us have been burned at one time or another. We have given our best, poured out our hearts, and loved without measure only to be rejected, shunned, or ignored.

Through my years in ministry, I've had a lot of chances to feel the pain of lost relationships. Whether through misunderstandings, offenses, or people simply moving on, I have felt the loss of friends and those to whom I gave myself. The long-term impact of these losses went undetected for years, but I eventually began to feel the effects of a heart gone cold.

As I prayed through this one day, I realized I needed a heart transplant. I saw where my emotions were frozen and even hardened out of necessity. It had been easier to simply shut down emotionally to avoid hurt, rejection, or the fear of rejection and I hadn't realized how much this was affecting me in my relationship with God.

"Why haven't I been able to feel love from You the way I used to?" I asked Him. He replied, *"Because you've said you don't need it!"*

His answer shocked me initially, but I quickly knew what He was referring to. In my journey of lost relationships, I had begun to believe that if I just stopped feeling so deeply about people, maybe it wouldn't hurt so much when they left. If I just didn't care quite as much maybe I could distance myself from those who may threaten to walk away.

Unfortunately, love can't be compartmentalized. When I shut out caring for others, I ended up shutting off my ability to give and receive love from the Lord, as well. My heart had become cold and indifferent and now it had hardened my heart in ways I never intended.

This is when I realized I needed a heart transplant. I had been trying to love others by myself. I thought that was good enough, but then I realized it wasn't. There was a greater Love that was much stronger and able to withstand the constant drain of unmet expectations and hopes unfulfilled that I experienced with others.

I asked Him, "How do I love with Your heart instead of mine?" I couldn't understand the difference, but I knew there must be one. Without hesitation He answered,

"When you can receive both praise as well as criticism from someone without it changing your heart towards them, then you will truly love as I do. I am not hurt by criticism and I don't need praise. Your self-protection and need for validation are what limits you from feeling and loving from My heart. When you can separate yourself from those tendencies, you will be able to love and to act from My heart with freedom and grace."

With those words, the revelation came. Then I truly understood -

Love is patient and kind; love does not envy or boast; it is not arrogant or rude. It does not insist on its own way;
it is not irritable or resentful; it does not rejoice at wrongdoing, but rejoices with the truth. Love bears all things, believes all things, hopes all things, endures all things. Love never ends.
1 Corinthians 13:4-8a

Lord, I want to truly love as You do. I give to You my own heart that is frail and weak. Heal me from past wounds that have hardened my heart and caused my love to grow cold. I desire to receive love and to give it in a life-giving way. I lay down the need to protect myself from pain and ask that You would stand guard at the gate of my heart so that Your love alone would rule. Come and give me the needed heart transplant so that I can love as You do with a pure love that asks nothing in return. In Jesus' name, amen.

Faith is The Fuel

And without faith it is impossible to please Him,
for whoever would draw near to God must believe that He exists
and that He rewards those who seek Him.
Hebrews 11:6

We often hear that "prayer changes things," but scripturally, it's not the power of prayer, but the faith behind it that brings results. "He touched their eyes, saying, 'According to your faith be it done to you'" (Matthew 9:29). It is not a matter of praying harder, louder, or longer. It's a matter of getting *God's heart* settled in *your own heart.*

The reason that faith is so important to God is because it is the evidence that we truly believe in who He is and in what He says. It is the evidence that we are not looking to ourselves, our situations, or other people to determine our future or outcome, but Him. It is the unwavering *knowing* that "He's got this!"

Faith in Him is the fuel of our prayers.

If we are unsure of what we are asking from Him, our spiritual gas tank is empty, and we will get nowhere. "But let him ask in faith, with no doubting, for the one who doubts is like a wave of the sea that is driven and tossed by the wind. For that person must not suppose that he will receive anything from the Lord; he is a double-minded man, unstable in all his way" (James 1:6-8).

When we come to His Word, He wants to reveal to us the heart of the Father, the mind of Christ, and the power of His Spirit. As each of these are established and nurtured in the secret place, our relationship with God deepens, our faith grows, and our prayers become powerful (James 2:23).

Before we can even begin to pray effectively, we must settle where our faith lies. Ultimately, our faith does not lie in *an* answer, but in *the* answer, God Himself. It is God's heart and character that are the bedrock of our faith. We don't have to know what an outcome might be as much as Who is behind it. When we truly know His heart for us, we will not question His ways, His means, or His methods. We'll simply trust Him.

If you are not in this place of confidence, start by emptying yourself of any fear or anxiety you are carrying. Get honest with God. Tell Him what you are thinking and share your doubts. As you recognize these ungodly beliefs and states of mind that clog up the pipeline of your faith, you can then allow Him to deal with them.

Faith is secured when you are sure of what God says about a matter. Romans 10:17 states that faith is established when we hear God's Word. This can come through reading Scripture, worship, listening to a good teaching, hearing testimonies, or remembering His faithfulness in the past. Find what it is that helps you build your own faith in Him and fill up your faith tank before attempting to go anywhere.

Lord, I confess to You the doubts and fears I have regarding_____ (name any specific doubt or fear). Forgive my unbelief about these issues and teach me Your truth that I might come to You in absolute faith and trust. I recognize that I need to build up my faith by _____ (name the ways in which you will actively build your faith.)

I want to please You. Fill me with a greater revelation of Your love, an increase of wisdom and discernment through the mind of Christ, and a tangible demonstration of the Spirit's power at work in my life. Help me to establish a solid foundation of faith in my life that will be unshakeable. In Jesus' name, amen.

THE PROMISE KEEPS US

As you wait for God's answers and learn how to build your faith in Him, there is something else you must settle - His promises. Maybe you have sung that "…*His promises are true, Yes and Amen…*" but do you really live like they are? More importantly, what are His specific promises to *you*? Do you have a record of what He has spoken to your heart concerning your life and purpose? Have you heard His voice at a personal level that has convinced you of His plan for your life?

This is my comfort in my affliction,
that Your promise gives me life.
Psalm 119:50

No unbelief made him waver concerning the promise of God,
but he grew strong in his faith as he gave glory to God.
Romans 4:20

The Greek word for promise means "a promised good or blessing." God's promise to us is a declaration of His intention to "graciously bestow a gift." This is a good thing and it is guaranteed, for God can't lie (Hebrews 6:18). He makes promises to us because He wants the best for us. He has assumed responsibility for our well-being and has provided everything we need to succeed (2 Peter 1:3). He is so committed to His covenant with us that He has promised to undergird us, support us, and empower us to do all and be all He has intended.

Promises are written in His Word, but they can also be spoken to us in prayer or through a word of encouragement. The gifts of the Spirit (1 Corinthians 12) are given in order to encourage one another and build one another's faith. They are given to remind us of the promises of God.

A word of prophecy is one of these gifts. It's a reminder from heaven that He cares for you and is working on your behalf. It is simply hearing God's voice and then speaking it out. It is available to anyone who lives by God's Spirit. The apostle Paul states how important this gift is to the Body of Christ.

Pursue love, and earnestly desire the spiritual gifts, especially that you may prophesy ... the one who prophesies speaks to people for their upbuilding and encouragement and consolation.
1 Corinthians 14:1,3

The gift of prophecy gives voice to God's promises for us. Through words of prophecy, we can receive a fresh reminder of His love, care, and commitment to us through a supernatural utterance of God's heart. Whether receiving a prophetic word through another brother or sister in Christ or a perfect stranger, these words will build our faith and keep us focused on God's promise.

The key is to write them down "…so that you may not be sluggish, but imitators of those who through faith and patience inherit the promises" (Hebrews 6:11). When you know a promise is given to you, it's critical to write it down and visit it. Often!

Obviously, there are some prerequisites to seeing God's promises fulfilled. Our obedience to what He has already told us, our pursuit of holiness, the posture of our heart, and our belief in His Word are all factors in seeing these promises come to pass.

In my younger years, I kept a journal of all of God's promises for me and my family. I referred to it almost daily and it strengthened my faith and encouraged my soul. I have also learned to write down answered prayers and breakthroughs so that I can remember what He has already done for me.

The enemy will do all he can to make us forget. Don't let him! Determine to keep a log of what God has spoken to you and reflect on it until it is written on your heart. The promises of God are powerful when we steward them well and share them with others.

Father, I thank You for Your promises which are "Yes" and "Amen." I thank You for Your written Word as well as the prophetic word that You speak over me. Open my eyes and ears to receive Your word for my life and remind me to repeat it out loud and share it with others. I pray that the fulfillment of these promises would bring great encouragement to those around me and strengthen our resolve to trust You for even greater measure of what You want to pour out in the days to come. May I be a voice of Your promise to others and declare aloud Your love! In Jesus' name, amen.

THE SECRET
of a
SANCTIFIED LIFE

And I will vindicate the holiness of My great Name,
which has been profaned among the nations,
and which you have profaned among them.
And the nations will know that I am the Lord,
declares the Lord God, when through you I vindicate
My holiness before their eyes.

Ezekiel 36:23

They Are Attracted
to Holiness

A Messenger once came to me in a dream and said, "...they are attracted to holiness." I knew he was speaking of the angels. He was telling me that the angels are attracted to holiness. From eternity's end they have been before His throne, worshiping Him in His holiness.

Holy, holy, holy is the LORD Almighty; the whole earth is full of His glory. At the sound of their voices the doorposts and thresholds shook, and the temple was filled with smoke.
Isaiah 6:3-4

Angels were created and designed to proclaim the holiness of God. When they come before God's holiness, they can't stop declaring it to one another. The seraphim and cherubim cover their faces and feet as they fall down before Him, taken by the beauty of His holiness.

These heavenly beings are not just some mindless robotic creatures taking orders, but living creations able to feel and respond to God's presence, just like us (Luke 2:13, James 2:19, Revelation 12:17).

The angels are attracted to God's holiness because it is His holiness that separates Him from all other beings.

His holiness is what makes Him distinct from everything else; it is the essence of His transcendence. This is why He invites us to be holy as He is holy. He knows that walking in holiness will attract heaven!

He has raised up a horn of salvation for us in the house of His servant David...to rescue us from the hand of our enemies, and to

enable us to serve Him without fear in holiness and
righteousness before Him all our days.
Luke 1:69, 74-75

We create an atmosphere around us by how we think, talk, and act. We can attract either light or darkness by what we carry in our hearts and minds. We have an opportunity every day to attract angelic assistance and the power of heaven. It will be determined by our obedience to God's Word and the purity of our heart. The spiritual realm is real and very active. Our Father has provided help for us and given the angels charge over us. Yet, they will only respond according to our words and actions.

Bless the Lord, O you His angels, you mighty ones who do His
word, obeying the voice of His word.
Psalm 103:20

It's up to you to walk in such a way that will open the way for angelic assistance that will usher in a tangible evidence of God's presence in your life. Determine to pursue a purity of heart and passion for the holiness of God. Pray that it will become so familiar to you that the angels won't be able to stay away from you!

Lord God, I worship You in the beauty of Your holiness. I acknowledge that it is Your holiness that sets You apart from all others and I join with the angels who cry out, "Holy are You!" I thank You for giving me access before Your throne and I ask that You would fill me afresh with Your perfect love and perfect ways. May I be a fragrance and aroma that would attract heaven and compel the angels to rejoice and act on my behalf. May all who seek You know that holiness is love perfected and not to fear You, but draw near to You in reverence and awe. For Your glory and fame, forever, amen.

HOLINESS DISARMS
THE ENEMY

Why is the holiness of God so powerful? There is a correlation between being holy and disarming the enemy's attacks. We've been taught to quote scriptures and sing praises in order to overcome the enemy's assault. But, how many times have we considered the power of God's holiness to totally disarm the attacks? Do we realize the ability of God's holiness within us to shield and protect us from our spiritual adversary?

In Zechariah 3, Joshua the high priest was standing before the throne of God and Satan was at his right hand accusing him. Joshua was under attack and he came to God for help. Joshua was filthy. His dirty garments were the result of the iniquity and sin that permeated his life. However, the Lord rebuked the Accuser and told those attending nearby to take off Joshua's sin-stained garments.

Then He said, "Behold, I have taken your iniquity away from you, and I will clothe you with pure vestments" (v.4). Those pure vestments represented the righteousness and holiness of God. Because of Joshua's posture of heart in coming before the throne of grace, God cleansed him of his sin and that which the Accuser had brought against him. Given a clean slate, the Accuser now had no case against Joshua. He was now covered in the righteousness of God, thus totally disarming his Accuser.

Because we have now been declared priests unto the Lord, this promise is also for us (Revelation 1:6). When we stand in the righteousness of Christ, the enemy has NO hold on us.

God has given us access into the holy place knowing that this is *the place where the enemy can't touch us.*

This is not automatic, however. We must approach the throne of grace just as Joshua did. Hebrews tells us we can come with boldness and confidence because of Christ's sacrificial love for us (Hebrews 10:19-23). We don't come because we deserve it. We come because we believe in what Christ did for us (Galatians 3:6). We become holy, not by doing things better or trying harder, but by fixing our eyes on Him and partaking of His divine nature (2 Timothy 1:9). He calls us to be like Him in holiness and righteousness because of the power it produces.

Holiness is not a set of rules but a power source from heaven.

So, I will show My greatness and My holiness and make Myself *known in the eyes of many nations.* *Then they will know that I am the Lord.* *Ezekiel 38:23*

Holiness grows when we are willing to do whatever it takes to be right with God and others. It is this posture of surrender that the enemy cannot withstand. Determine to access the holiness of God by coming before the throne of grace to be cleansed, restored, and renewed. Trade in your filthy rags and stand secure in the righteousness of Christ.

Lord Jesus, thank You for giving me access to the throne of grace *through the work of the cross. I now come and ask to be cleansed* *of my sin in order to embrace Your gift of righteousness in my life.* *I want to be holy, even as You are holy. Fill me with Your truth and* *silence my Accuser. Thank You for helping me stand secure in this* *place of freedom and peace. Teach me to walk in the power of Your* *holiness. In Jesus' name, amen.*

HE HAS NO HOLD ON ME!

Not only is holiness a means of spiritual protection and a power source to disarm the enemy, it provides increased spiritual authority in our life. When we walk in true righteousness, we are free from anything the enemy might try to use against us. Jesus walked in this reality.

>...*for the ruler of this world is coming. He has no claim on me.*
>*John 14:30*

Jesus was not threatened by Satan because he had no "claim" on Jesus. Some Bible versions say Satan had no "hold" over Jesus. This is an amazing declaration because it provides the key to the kind of authority Jesus had over His spiritual adversary.

>...*but I do as the Father has commanded Me,*
>*so that the world may know that I love the Father.*
>*John 14:31*

Jesus would later tell Pilate that no one could take His life because He freely gave it (John 19:11). Regardless of how it appeared, Jesus exercised absolute freedom in His journey to the cross because He was totally free of anyone else's control or manipulation. There was nothing that Satan could hold over Jesus' head because Jesus walked in absolute obedience to His Father. He was in good standing!

This kind of freedom can only come as a result of total submission to the Father. What Jesus did, we can do. He walked the earth as a man in order to demonstrate for us what is possible when we abide in the Father, just as He did.

Jesus demonstrated that it is possible to overcome every scheme of the enemy when we walk in obedience to the Father and in true righteousness. When we obey His voice without delay, all of heaven backs us up and nothing is impossible.

A fully-surrendered life is no match for the devil.

Every day, we can choose to embrace this attitude and determine to walk as Jesus did. We can live without anything hanging over our heads or threatening our destiny. When we yield to the Father and obey His voice, there's nothing the enemy can do to stop us. We will be backed by the authority of our Father and the resources of heaven.

Search your heart and allow the Holy Spirit to reveal anything that the enemy may be threatening you with. Consider if there is any validity in the charge and take it before the Lord in prayer. Just as Jesus did, avoid defending yourself (Mark 15:5), and simply determine to submit your life to God in order to take care of any charges that have been brought against you. Know that as you pursue a life of obedience and holiness, you will experience greater and greater freedom and spiritual authority because of heaven's favor. Trust that your Heavenly Father will shower you with His grace and divinely enable you to accomplish everything He has set out for you to do and be.

Father, I want to have the same testimony as Jesus in knowing that I am free of any charge brought against me by my enemies. Search my heart and reveal anything I need to take care of. Cleanse my heart and mind and enable me to walk in right relationship with You and others so that I might be truly free. I desire to say with Jesus that the enemy has no hold on me! Thank You for empowering me by Your Spirit to walk as Jesus did and walk in freedom and joy. For Your sake and Your glory. Amen.

Come as the Angels Do

In a vision of the night, I had an angelic encounter where I was given a specific directive in how to come to the Father. I knew I was in the throne room of heaven. The angels spoke to me regarding my posture before the Father in prayer.

In the encounter, I saw and heard angels speak to me from the ground. I saw their faces on the floor speaking from the ground up – not from heaven-down.

One of them said to me, "Ask God what He wants at the beginning of your prayers…not at the end."

Even as I heard this, I sensed that all of heaven was standing ready to charge to the earth. They were in formation with swords drawn, waiting for the command to come. I was led to the Lord's Prayer (Matthew 6:9-13; Luke 11:2-4) since this is where His disciples asked Him how to pray. I noticed that it begins with an acknowledgement of God as our Father and then recognizes His holiness.

Our Father, which art in heaven, hallowed be Thy name.
Matthew 6:9

The last part of this prayer is what many of us focus on when contending for a breakthrough in prayer:

For thine is the kingdom, the power, and the glory,
for ever and ever. Amen.

Though this phrase is not included in all the modern translations, it was recorded in most ancient manuscripts, and has become a traditional ending to this famous prayer. As we cry out for deliverance from evil, we also declare the ultimate authority of Christ's kingdom.

Even so, the instruction given in my vision was specific. I was reminded of the importance of my heart posture when coming to the Father before the throne. I have often come with a warrior mentality, ready to take down whatever enemy is crossing my path! I quickly go to the last part of the Lord's Prayer, trying to make a case for my victory as I declare, "We win!"

However, this is what I realized needed to change. Rather than coming to prove my ability to fight, I needed to start in humble adoration and worship. My heart must start in humility before it can rise to victory. Before I can even address the battle, I must honor the King.

It all starts with face-down worship.

Intercession is not meant to be a power confrontation. It is an act of worship to the Lord acknowledging His rule and authority that has already secured the promise for us, our families, and our communities. I believe I saw and heard the angels on the floor representing the call to *humility* and an acknowledgment of God's *holiness.*

In Revelation, numerous pictures are given of the angelic host in worship around the throne, and in each instance, they are face down on the floor.

And I heard every creature in heaven and on earth and under the
earth and in the sea, and all that is in them, saying,
"To Him who sits on the throne and to the Lamb
be blessing and honor and glory and might forever and ever!"
And the four living creatures said, "Amen!"
and the elders fell down and worshiped.
Revelation 5:13-14

Even as we pray for things to change here on the earth so that they can reflect heaven's will and purpose, we must first come in humble adoration of our Ruler and King.

It is only when we are in the right posture that we carry the right authority.

How do you come before the Father in the secret place? What does it mean for you to come humbly and "face-down?" Before you start asking the Lord for answers or engaging in a fight, come as the angels do by simply humbling yourself in awe and worship.

Heavenly Father, I come before You face down in worship. I acknowledge that You alone are the One worthy of adoration and praise. I ask that You align my heart to Yours so that I can come in agreement with Your sovereign purposes. Rid me of any false humility or presumption and fill me with Your Spirit of truth. I yield to You my rights and claims, and surrender all I have and all I am. You are the Holy One and the only source that is pure, untainted, and perfect. I thank You for the power of Your holiness and I join the angels in heaven's worship that is eternal. For Jesus' sake, amen.

THE LATENT POWER
OF OBEDIENCE

*So, Jesus said to them, "Truly, truly, I say to you, the Son can do
nothing of His own accord, but only what He sees the Father
doing. For whatever the Father does, that the Son does likewise.
For the Father loves the Son and shows Him all that He himself is
doing. And greater works than these will He show Him,
so that you may marvel."*
John 5:19-20

Can you imagine the restraint Jesus must have had while here on earth? We read of the miracles He performed, but how many more did He walk away from out of His obedience to the Father? How many times did He want to stretch out His hand to raise the dead or demonstrate His power, and yet held back? In Mark 1:36-38, the disciples told Jesus everyone was looking for Him, but instead of staying and ministering to their needs, Jesus left in order to follow His Father's call to another city.

**Jesus was focused, not on demonstrating His power,
but on listening to His Father.**

There is a hidden power in obedience. Jesus restrained Himself at times because He knew that His power would only be perfected through obedience.

*Although He was a son, He learned obedience through what He
suffered. And being made perfect, He became the source of eternal
salvation to all who obey Him.*
Hebrews 5:8-9

53

Consider the results Jesus had in His obedience to the Father. It was in the latter part of His earthly ministry that Jesus raised Lazarus from the dead (John 11:43). Though He performed many miracles, it wasn't until several years into His ministry that He called His friend back to life in a dramatic fashion that stunned even His followers.

Jesus was tested as a man. He was tested in the wilderness by Satan and He won. His own Father disciplined Jesus for a higher purpose in bringing eternal salvation to all who believed in Him. Hebrews states Jesus had to learn obedience and it wasn't easy. He had to learn how to obey His Father just like we do.

Could it be that raising Lazarus from the dead came as a result of the obedience Jesus walked in? Could it be that Jesus demonstrated for us an obedience that opens doors to the miraculous? If we would walk in the same level of absolute surrender as Christ did, could we also expect to raise people from the dead!?

Truly, truly, I say to you, whoever believes in Me will also do the works that I do; and greater works than these will he do, because I am going to the Father.
John 14:12

What untold miracles and breakthroughs are possible for us who choose to walk in absolute obedience to the Father? What possibilities might there be in the simple act of following through on what God tells us to do?

What was the last thing God told you to do? Have you done it? What truths has He told you that you have yet to act upon? Whatever He has told you to say or to do, be assured He will help you accomplish them. Start with the willingness and ask Him to help you follow through.

Heavenly Father, I desire to live in daily communion with You. I desire to hear Your voice clearly and recognize what You are doing. I commit myself to walking in obedience to Your Word and ask that You would work in me to "...will and work for Your good pleasure" (Philippians 2:13). I thank You for the authority You give me as I walk in obedience to You. Show me today what You are doing and saying. I pray that I might be a vessel through which signs, wonders, and miracles can take place for Your glory and Your fame.
In Jesus' name, amen.

Who Are You?

The evil spirit answered them,
"Jesus I know, and Paul I recognize, but who are you?"
Acts 19:15

When the sons of Sceva tried to cast out devils, they thought they had the right recipe for success. They had watched the disciples of Jesus do it and they thought they could, as well. They said the right words and invoked the right name. However, it not only failed, but opened the door to demonic attack because of their pride and presumption. Though their outward actions may have seemed spiritual enough, their hearts were not right with God.

It's a natural tendency to try and discover the perfect checklist that will guarantee our prayers answered and problems solved. We can easily look at the success of others and simply try to imitate them. However, our journey with God has to be our own. And, it is not so much about *what* we do as much as *how* we do it.

Jesus is much more interested in our heart posture toward Him than our posturing before men.

The words of these self-righteous imposters had no meaning because their hearts were not right with God. Even if we try to employ the tools and techniques of others, we will be without power if we imitate them with no genuine faith of our own. We have to grow our own faith and it has to be real. Heaven knows the difference.

As you pursue a life of being right with God and right with others, be yourself and be real! Even as you are inspired by others, know that you are an original and not a copy. Even as you become more and more like Jesus, you will still be an original version and not a copy.

With social media prevalent in our culture, it is very easy to try and be like everyone else. We see what others say and do, and feel the need to follow suit in order to gain more followers or get more "likes." However, this can be a trap.

We can never measure our success by our Facebook profiles or our Twitter feeds. Our notoriety is much more important on the other side of the veil. What we do here is only temporary. Who we are in eternity's eyes will last forever.

Authenticity is greatly lacking today. The world is longing for the real thing, not a counterfeit. There are an increasing number of counterfeiters in the world and it's up to us to stand secure in that which is true, real, and lasting.

I am writing these things to you about those who are trying to lead you astray. As for you, the anointing you received from Him remains in you, and you do not need anyone to teach you. But as His anointing teaches you about all things and as that anointing is real, not counterfeit—just as it has taught you, remain in Him.
1 John 2:26-27

If you want to fulfill God's plan for your life and see the authority of Christ demonstrated through your life, pray for a first-hand revelation and encounter that is yours. You can learn from others, but determine to walk out your faith and understanding in the secret place with the Lord before presuming to work for Him in public.

What you do in public is fed by what you do in private. As you daily fill yourself with God's Word and take time in His presence, there will be an overflow that will pour out without effort and with great power. When you do this, your spiritual enemies will not only know who you are, but Whose you are!

Father, I come with the desire to develop an ongoing first-hand relationship with You. I don't want to be a copy, but an authentic representative of Christ. I trust that You are working in me and through me to walk and talk as Jesus did in order that others will know You. Thank You for the anointing You have given me to recognize Your truth and be faithful to Your Word. In Christ's name, amen.

THE POWER OF
YOUR OWN HISTORY

W e may love the Bible story of speaking life to dead things found in Ezekiel 37, but we have totally missed a key element in the reason for this supernatural resurrection! The Lord brought Ezekiel to a valley of dry bones and told him to prophesy life to them.

Prophesy to these bones and say to them, "Dry bones, hear the word of the LORD! This is what the Sovereign LORD says to these bones: I will make breath enter you, and you will come to life. I will attach tendons to you and make flesh come upon you and cover you with skin; I will put breath in you, and you will come to life. Then you will know that I am the LORD."
Ezekiel 36:4-6

We have used this reference as a formula for declaring life into dead situations, relationships, and various issues in our life which need resurrection power. Though faith is usually exercised in this pronouncement of life, I see another, more important factor that is behind the success of Ezekiel's command. This was not a demonstration of prophetic authority but a powerful result of a prophetic life.

Ezekiel had a history with God.

We need to realize that Ezekiel came to that valley with a history – an amazing journey of surrender, radical obedience, and a sanctified life. It is this key ingredient which makes Ezekiel's pronouncement so incredible and the single most important ingredient that is desperately needed today in the Church. Without this ingredient, our prophetic pronouncements may be sincere and heartfelt, but lacking in power.

What is Ezekiel's history? After Assyria conquered Israel, the Jews were scattered, and Ezekiel lived with the other Jewish exiles in Babylonia. They were lost, angry, and without cause. Though he was from a priestly line, the Lord called Ezekiel as a prophet to his people. Unfortunately, God not only told him that the people wouldn't listen to him (2:4), but that things would get worse before they got better! The Jews would see Jerusalem fall before they were ready for God's intervention. Ezekiel's job was to warn his brethren about the impending destruction and call them back to God. In doing so, God asked Ezekiel to do some extremely insane things!

Ezekiel was to be a signpost to the people (Ezekiel 12:11), meaning that he was supposed to demonstrate God's messages in very specific ways. He was not to simply speak prophetic words, but to live a prophetic life. By demonstrating humility and a willingness to follow at all costs, people around him would see God's will in action.

Consider the things Ezekiel was asked to do:

- Eat a scroll of mourning and lament to have God's heart for intercession (3:1-4).
- Be tied up with ropes in his own home and unable to speak until the Lord allowed him (3:25-27).
- Lay on his right side for 390 days and then on his left side for 40 days to symbolize Israel's years of rebellion (Chapter 4).
- Shave his head and beard, which was usually unlawful for a Jew (Chapter 5).
- Prophesy death and destruction to his brethren (11:10-13).
- Pack his belongings and hand dig through the wall to demonstrate what would happen to the Israelites in captivity (12:1-6).

As if these things didn't already test Ezekiel's resolve to humble himself before the Lord in complete surrender and obedience, he was told one more heart-wrenching command. The Lord told Ezekiel that

He would take his wife "with one blow" to be a sign to Israel of what would happen to their beloved city, Jerusalem. Ezekiel was told he couldn't even mourn her death (24:15-16).

Here was a prophet who had faithfully obeyed every command of the Lord, willing to suffer ridicule, scrutiny, and to prophesy doom and destruction to his fellow Jews. Now, he was told that the love of his life would be taken from him as a sign. Scripture doesn't indicate what Ezekiel's initial response was. All we can assume is that he faithfully trusted the Lord's directives just as before. The next chapter simply picks up with the next word that the Lord gave to him.

It is just three chapters later that we finally get to the valley of the dry bones. This opportunity to see the power of God demonstrated before his eyes came after years of obedience and faithfulness to God's Word. It was not just the *prophet* Ezekiel who stood before those dry bones, but the *man* Ezekiel. This was someone who had a history with his God, living out every request and following every directive he was given. This is the key ingredient that gave him the authority to speak to those dry bones in the valley of death. He had already been there and knew what to do.

Because he had faithfully demonstrated humility, surrender, and faith in God through the years, those bones immediately responded to his words and a vast army stood before him full of resurrection power!

Because of his life of obedience and faithfulness, the man Ezekiel had the authority to raise the dead.

I believe this is where we are in the Church today. We have a huge valley of dry bones before us in our communities, cities, and our nation. We see biblical values dying, the decay of morals and absolutes, as well as a complete absence of the fear of the Lord. We desperately need supernatural intervention, the power of resurrection life, and a revival of passion for the Lord.

Though we know that God can raise the dead to life, the question is, can our prophetic declarations be backed up by a personal history with God? Do our lives reflect consistent surrender and absolute obedience to what He's already said? Have we so focused on the formulas of words or presumed rights to spiritual authority that we have totally missed the most important ingredient? The strongholds that we face today and the principalities that are threatening our communities and our nation will not be overcome by a power confrontation. It will not be a test of wills or the level of passion or the hours of prayer that will determine the outcome.

The enemies of God will be defeated by a holy and humble people who have demonstrated the rule of God through their lives and practices. It is a righteous life that will totally disarm the enemy and release the power to bring new life. These are not just values, but heart issues that must be tested and tried, just as they were for Ezekiel. I pray that the words God spoke to Ezekiel about Israel would be true for us today:

Then the nations will know that I am the Lord,
declares the Sovereign Lord, when I am proved holy
through you before their eyes.
Ezekiel 26:23

Father, I desire to walk with resurrection authority in my life! I want to have the testimony of Ezekiel in being faithful and true to Your Word, even when it's costly. Forgive me when I have not obeyed what You have spoken. Grant me a willing and obedient heart to follow Your commands and trust You with the outcomes. Teach me how to speak life to the dead areas of my life and those around me. Make me a vessel of Your power so that others can come to know You are the Way, the Truth, and the Life. In Jesus' name, amen.

EMPOWERED
THROUGH SUBMISSION

Submission is not a very popular term these days. Our knee-jerk reaction is to see the term as negative and oppressing. Perhaps it's more so for women who have traditionally been either ignored or suppressed both in the world as well as in the church.

My own journey through the years has been marked by struggles to "submit" to other leaders, especially in the church. In hindsight, I'm grateful for each and every relationship that challenged me. Each one became an iron-sharpening tool in my life to cut away my own selfishness, ambition, and pride. The Lord knew exactly what I needed to experience in order to understand His heart regarding healthy spiritual authority.

The importance of embracing spiritual authority is tested most when it comes to prayer. How we view and honor the authorities in our lives will greatly impact the effectiveness of our prayers.

We will have no spiritual authority in heaven if we do not honor and submit to our spiritual authorities on earth.

It's a commandment and one that we dare not reject simply because we've been wounded.

Let every person be subject to the governing authorities. For there is no authority except from God, and those that exist have been instituted by God. Therefore, whoever resists the authorities resists what God has appointed, and those who resist will incur judgment.
Romans 13:1-3

One of the secrets to embracing this command with joy is to realize that God asks us to honor the authorities in our lives, regardless of whether we like them, their personalities, or even their decisions. He is telling us to submit to them because of their role and function in our lives.

In cases where spiritual authorities are involved in known sin, heresy, or disobedience to the Word of God, godly oversight and intervention is needed. In most cases, however, our grievances against leaders are based on differences of opinion or varying interpretations of the Word. Even more, it is personal offenses or misunderstandings that create the biggest rifts and lack of unity when it comes to honoring spiritual authorities.

I have had many opportunities in my life to be hurt, rejected, misunderstood, and mistreated by spiritual authorities. I believe anyone to whom God wants to give spiritual authority will be tested in this. He is watching to see how we respond to those in authority over us, especially when we don't agree with them.

Our human nature tends to think God's ultimate goal is to fix a problem or prove a point. It's not. His ultimate goal is to sanctify our hearts. We are usually so preoccupied with the need to get spiritual authorities to agree with us or change their views, we ignore the posture of our own hearts and our ultimate trust in God to have the final word. Even when addressing valid concerns, our attitude and perspective will be critical if we want to see God have His way.

In my own marriage, I've had to deal with the temptation to coerce my husband into agreeing with me. Even when I thought he was wrong, the Lord taught me the power of submission. When I would surrender my need for validation and submit things to the Lord, it opened the way for the Holy Spirit to move and act. My husband would no longer hear my nagging voice, but the voice of the Holy Spirit. In my surrendered state, I would also hear more clearly. This would consistently bring us to the place of seeing God's perspective together over our own and come into greater agreement and unity.

Commit your way to the Lord; trust in Him and He will do this:
He will make your righteous reward shine like the dawn,
your vindication like the noonday sun.
Psalm 37:5-6

By honoring God's Word and submitting to His final authority, I have been able to let go of any tendency to control or manipulate leaders in my life.

I have found the greatest freedom when I lay down my right to be right.

I come to the point of no longer needing to prove myself, my call, my gift, or my spiritual authority. These are all validated through the fruit of my life, not the persistence of my pleas. This is what it means to be empowered through submission.

As we pray for various leaders in our lives it is critical that we honor them and seek to support them through our words and actions. We will have no authority in prayer to see leaders fulfill their assignment and succeed if we curse them on the side. God WILL have the final say, if we just do our part.

Lord Jesus, I thank You for the spiritual authorities You have placed in my life (name one or two that have a significant place in your life). I honor the role they have, and I pray that they would have a revelation of Your love and an encounter with Your grace. Forgive me for any attitude of criticism or judgment against them that has dishonored You. I pray that I would display Your kindness and goodness instead of criticism or blame (Romans 2:4). I speak blessing upon them so that they may accomplish and fulfill all that You have ordained. I place my faith in You as the final Authority in all things. In Jesus' name, amen.

GROWING
in
IN GRACE

And now I commend you to God and to the word of His grace, which is able to build you up and to give you the inheritance among all those who are sanctified.

Acts 20:32

You Have a Delightful Inheritance

Psalms 16:5-6 is my life verse:

The Lord is my chosen portion and my cup;
You hold my lot. The lines have fallen for me in pleasant places;
indeed, I have a beautiful inheritance.

This simple scripture outlines a beautiful picture of grace and how God has already worked it into the very fabric of our lives so that we can walk from a place of rest and well-being. When we walk in His grace, we will not strive or be driven to succeed. There will be an ease to what we do because we are doing exactly what He has planned for us. As we learn to recognize the healthy boundaries He has provided for us, we can walk in this grace and see tremendous fruit. It's only when we go outside those parameters that stress and weariness become evident.

Realize the power of these verses to secure your own place with Him and determine to walk in grace and not in striving.

He is my CHOSEN PORTION. "Portion" is that which I possess and inherit. It is everything I need in life. By this statement, I am choosing to make Him Lord, place Him first, and trust His dealings with me.

He is my CUP. This means He is the one who holds my life and everything He has for me in the palm of His hand. He alone knows exactly what I have been created for and He has made precise arrangements ahead of time for me to walk in this grace.

He holds my LOT. This is no guessing game or random approach. God has very specific plans for me! He knows ahead of time what I will choose and will work with me as I find my way. Even when I make mistakes, His loving kindness will draw me back into His perfect plan.

The LINES are unseen boundaries that He has established for my safety as well as for my success. Just as a loving shepherd provides a fence for his flock so that the enemy cannot enter, so God provides boundaries that will keep us in His grace. This has to do with how we use our time, what we focus our attention on, and who we spend our time with. These are things that can either produce good fruit or produce stress, all depending on whether we stay in the boundaries of His grace.

They have fallen for me in PLEASANT PLACES. God's intention is always to enlarge us and bless us, never to limit or hinder us. The boundaries in our lives are for our good so that we can operate in His grace and not go outside those parameters. If we submit to the boundary lines He has established, it will be pleasant, enjoyable, and good!

I have a BEAUTIFUL INHERITANCE because He is the One who has been planning and preparing me to receive the fullness of His promises in my life. He is daily working to make sure that I succeed and that I can enjoy my full inheritance in life, in the spiritual as well as in the natural.

Consider the boundaries in your own life. How are you spending your time and is it giving you joy and rest? What are you focusing your attention on? Is it producing good fruit? How many people are you relating to and what kind of fruit is coming from those relationships? As you seek to walk in God's grace and not in self-effort, allow the Holy Spirit to reveal any way in which you have gone outside His boundaries of grace. Determine to make any adjustment needed and realize that His desire for you is to be at peace. He is not a Task Master but a loving Shepherd who deeply cares for you.

Heavenly Father, please reveal to me any area in which I am striving in my flesh and not walking in Your grace. I will make the adjustments You show me. Enable me by Your Spirit to establish a new standard of rest and well-being so that I can be at my very best in reflecting Your heart and purposes to those around me. I thank You for giving me healthy boundaries and for establishing my walk. I trust You and praise You for the inheritance You have given me. You are a Good Father and I love You. In Jesus' name, amen.

A Task Master Called Performance

In recent years I hit a wall. I recognized the enemy of my soul and how he was slowly draining the life from me. I missed it for so long because he masqueraded as a champion of spiritual pursuit.

Instead, I found he was a task master called Performance. I allowed him access through my own need for achievement. His constant chatter in my head to "do more," "try this," or "do that" wore me out. I finally said, "Enough!"

Here is my personal paraphrase of Romans 6:11-12:

"In the same way, count yourselves dead to fleshly ambition and Performance, but alive to God in Christ Jesus. Therefore, do not let Performance, Production, or 'I Should' reign in your mind and emotions so that you obey their pressure to succeed. Do not offer your thoughts, time, and attention to these task masters in hopes of recognition, validation, or fame, but rather offer yourselves to God as One who has been brought from death to life. Surrender yourselves to Him as His son and daughter who is already recognized, esteemed, and worthy in His eyes. For Performance shall no longer be your master, because you are not under his rule and expectations but under God's grace" (Romans 6:11-14).

I have always been a "doer" and one who wants to accomplish great things for the Lord. There is certainly no sin in this, but our motivation can so easily be skewed if there's any hint of insecurity or doubt involved. Our Accuser knows how to take advantage of even our best qualities in order to immobilize us.

The voices in our head sound like us. They speak in first person. Many times, however, it's our spiritual adversary trying to convince us to take on his yoke and get out from underneath God's covering of grace.

God has promised me boundaries of grace that keep me secure, confident, and able to receive the fruit of faithfulness (Psalm 16:5-6). As I lean into His voice, and not my own or the enemy's, I can be assured of a delightful inheritance! I can't earn my inheritance – only receive it! The key is to shut off those voices in your head and replace them with God's truth. Revisit the words He has spoken to you previously and determine to live from a place of rest and peace, not striving and anxiety.

Do not allow Performance to rule you. He is never satisfied.

Our pursuit should never be what we try to produce or attempt to prove. Recognize the voice of Performance whispering in your ear and turn him off. Listen to the silence. The Father is speaking and calling you to come aside and lay down your striving. As Performance dies, Grace will be reborn. What the Father wants to do in and through you will become an expression of relationship with Him, not something you've worked for or achieved by your own willpower. Become a vessel of His Grace and not a slave to the task master of Performance.

I thank You, Father, for the boundaries of grace that You have established in my life. I choose now to lay down my own efforts to prove myself worthy or accomplish more than what You have ordained at this time. I say to those voices of Performance in my head, "I will not listen to you!" I listen, instead, to the Shepherd of my soul Who is looking out for me and extending His grace for each day. I will only do what You tell me to do and only say what You tell me to say. No more and no less. Amen!

SONSHIP – THE HIGHEST CALL

The Spirit Himself bears witness with our spirit that we
are children of God, and if children, then heirs –
heirs of God and fellow heirs with Christ.
Romans 8:16-17a

When I first began to understand the prophetic gifting I carried, I felt empowered. After years of feeling like my voice wasn't being heard, I finally felt qualified to speak. My journey of hearing the Father's voice and helping others to know Him better became an exciting adventure as my confidence grew. Through the fruit of the gift and the affirmation of others, I felt emboldened to hear and speak God's Word.

Then I came through a season where the Lord was teaching me what it meant to be His daughter. Not an ordained minister, pastor's wife, or prophet. Just…daughter. He reminded me that before I was anything else, I was His daughter. He also reminded me that one day the gifts will cease, but I will still be His daughter. As I was debating how the prophetic mantle and authority fit into all of this, He took me to Hebrews 1:1-2.

Long ago, at many times and in many ways, God spoke to our
fathers by the prophets, but in these last days **He has spoken to us**
by His Son, *whom He appointed the Heir of all things,*
through whom also He created the world.

There it was. Jesus was the perfect example of the highest position we can have with the Father. He was a son! Though He was God in the flesh and operated on the earth in all the spiritual gifts, His greatest role and position was that of His Father's Son.

I realized that my prayers and declarations to Him were not dependent on me being a recognized five-fold prophetic minister, but on being His daughter. Being a son or daughter of the King is the highest position anyone can have!

Not only does Jesus demonstrate the power of being a son of the Most High God, He also represented the power of being an heir. Only a son or daughter can receive an inheritance. We have been given authority and access because we are heirs. It all started in the Garden when God gave Adam and Eve authority over the earth to steward and rule over it. Life in the Garden was for His sons and daughters – not for five-fold ministers.

This is the same reality He is teaching many of us today – to remember who we are as sons and daughters, so we can fulfill our original mandate here on the earth. You don't have to be a prophet, pastor, teacher, or have a position in the church. You don't have to have a title, for you have already been given a call and mantle more powerful than anything else. You are His son! You are His daughter!

The gifts of God are powerful. But, perhaps they are only necessary if there aren't any sons or daughters around.

Father, I thank You for calling me Your son/daughter. I thank You that "sonship" is the highest call I will ever have on my life. I desire to walk in the reality of being Your heir. Forgive me if I have placed more importance on my role, position, or title than I have in being your son/daughter. Renew my mind so that I can see the favor and blessing of living as Your son/daughter and help me to represent You well. In Jesus' name, amen.

HURRY UP
AND WAIT!

One of the hardest things to do is to wait on God. We are told that patience is a fruit of the Spirit, yet, it is one of the hardest attributes of Christ to practice. Since it is a fruit, we cannot try to have it; it must be an overflow of His presence and peace residing within us. In our frustration, we sometimes ask God to give us patience – not realizing that we have just given Him permission to give us a reason to need it!

It can be even harder when we feel like we have heard a word from the Lord regarding a promise and when it doesn't appear, we wonder why. It can feel like He is dangling a carrot before us, only to yank it away at the last moment – just to frustrate us. Obviously, this is not His heart. He does not delight in delay. What He does, is purposefully direct every step we take in order for us to know the extent and depth of His love for us.

Therefore, the Lord waits to be gracious to you,
and therefore He exalts Himself to show mercy to you.
For the Lord is a God of justice;
blessed are all those who wait for Him.
Isaiah 30:18

On one occasion I was struggling while waiting on God to answer a prayer I had been praying for a long time. I felt that I knew His plan for me, but it just wasn't happening the way I thought. I had been trying to understand His reasoning, when He gently exhorted me:

"Wanda, you've been trusting My *plans* for you, but I want you to trust My *love* for you."

Wow. He hit a bullseye on my heart that I didn't even know was there. I had been so focused on the "what," I hadn't been focusing on "Who." It was another reminder that my faith must rest in Him as a loving Father, not in the things He promises. As a result, my perspective changed, and I had renewed faith in the waiting.

When we were in the process of looking for a new home in the country, after years of waiting in a small house in the suburbs, I felt that He had given me assurance of providing us our dream home. After months of looking to no avail, I was discouraged. I began to feel as if He was holding out on us; we just couldn't find anything. He had told us to make a list of everything we wanted. We had done this with previous homes with great results. But, now I began to wonder if maybe, this time, we had asked for too much.

I was having a mental battle with this one day as I was cleaning our bedroom. I was somewhat frustrated at God, wanting Him to give me an answer for this seemingly unnecessary delay in His promise. As I bent down to pick up something underneath our bed, I found a penny. I had to smile, since this had been a recurring incident for about two years - finding pennies in the most unusual places. Every time, I felt the Lord was reminding me of the message inscribed on the coin: "In God We Trust." Every time I found a penny I knew He was reminding me to trust in Him. This time, however, there was an added message that caught me totally unawares as I had bent down to find this hidden treasure:

"Wanda, I'm not hiding this house *from* you. I'm hiding it *for* you."

Immediately, my heart skipped a beat. In one split second, my heart went from feeling ignored and deprived, to feeling excited and even giddy. Suddenly, I felt His excitement and joy concerning our new home. I knew that the only reason we hadn't found it yet was because He was planning and preparing something so special for us, He had to hide it away for a special reveal. From that moment on, my faith soared and I knew that He would keep His promise, regardless of the wait time.

Just a few weeks later, we found our dream home! Not only was it everything we had asked for, but more – much more. It also came about in a surprising way that confirmed the word the Father had spoken to me.

It turned out that the only reason we found the house was because, only the day before we viewed it, the price was dropped by $40,000! The owner had this beautiful country property on the market for months without any buyer. He had just dropped the price when I "found" it on my realty app the same day. Because the property had been listed in the higher price bracket, it had been "hidden" from us – until the precise moment we were ready to see it and say "Yes!" Not only were we the first potential buyers to see the house at the reduced price, several others who were scheduled right after us, never showed up. Months later, the (Christian) owner would tell us that he knew we were the ones meant to live in that house.

Our Father loves to provide for us. He has good things in store for us. But, this often means we need to wait for it. This has been a recurring theme throughout my own journey as He has continually challenged my faith with opportunities to wait – and trust. Every time, I have grown more in love with Him as a Father who truly delights in fulfilling His promises to His sons and daughters, His heirs.

The saying, "Good things come to those who wait" may not come from the Bible, but it is certainly a kingdom principle. When we get a revelation of His love for us and are convinced of His faithfulness, we can be assured of His rewards and can confidently wait for them.

I believe that I shall look upon the goodness of the Lord in the land of the living! Wait for the Lord; be strong, and let your heart take courage; wait for the Lord!
Psalm 27:13-14

Heavenly Father, thank You for Your loving kindness and Your desire to fill me with good things. I trust in You this day to fulfill Your purposes for me, even if it means waiting. Thank You for giving me Your peace and patience through the power of the Holy Spirit. Enable me to live from this place of absolute confidence in Your plans to prosper me and give me a hope and a future. Thank You for calling me Your heir, qualified as Your son/daughter to receive the abundance of Your house. In Jesus' name, amen.

He Wants to Capture Your Heart

I woke up hearing the words to a popular chorus, *"It's extravagant. It doesn't make sense - the way You love us, the way You love us."* I knew He wanted to remind me of something.

I have always been an overachiever by nature and have been prone to want to "fix" things. Whether it's myself or others, I am always striving to make things better (at least from my perspective). Though my intentions may be good, this mindset gets me into trouble. I go beyond His boundaries of grace, get into things I shouldn't, and make mistakes. I am hardest on myself. I asked the Lord once how He deals with the issues I get stuck in. He said, "I'm not driven by agenda (like you are). My goal and My passion is YOU"!

I was immediately convicted. For me, it's about getting things done, making things right, making people happy. For Him, it's all about relationship and the posture of our hearts. He reminded me of the story of the woman caught in adultery (John 8:3-10). When He bent down in the dirt to write, He wasn't thinking about the law...or the Pharisees...or how to fix things. He was thinking about her.

He was thinking of how to capture her heart, not corner her in her sin.

His ultimate goal and desire is always, first and foremost, to be in relationship with us. Fixing things and getting things done are afterthoughts to Him. He is bent on us. He is bent on you.

Even when we have made mistakes and failed, His redeeming grace is gentle and fixated on connecting with our heart. He knows that until our hearts are truly His, no standard of righteousness will keep us close to Him. He doesn't *make* us want Him. He longs for us to come to Him with a free will and hungry heart.

The woman caught in adultery must have been shocked and somewhat dumbfounded as to how to respond. It shouldn't have been so easy! Yet, here was a man who knew exactly what she had done, but, unlike her accusers, was not intent on making a federal case of it. He simply shared His heart for her and exhorted her to move past it.

He wants our hearts before He wants our good behavior.

As a young parent, I learned this truth as I was driving in the car one day, frustrated that my daughter's behavior was far below my expectations of her. In the midst of my mental tirade, the Father interrupted me. "Don't worry about training her behavior. Train her heart."

That revelation changed me. I realized that a truly good parent will focus much more on a child's heart and motivation than on their outward behavior. Behaviors come and go, but the heart is central.

The good person out of the good treasure of his heart produces good, and the evil person out of his evil treasure produces evil, for out of the abundance of the heart his mouth speaks.
Luke 6:45

Know that your Heavenly Father is a great parent. His heart is constantly bent towards you. Your sin or failures don't compare to the amazing love and grace He has for you. He is not trying to corner you in any sin or weakness. Rather, He is waiting for you to trust His heart that is full of unconditional love so that you can move past it. He is bending down towards you, captured by you as His child. Receive it. This is the kind of capture that will set your heart free.

The Victory is Greater Than the Pain

These were the words the Lord gave me when I was feeling the burden of a painful situation. I was hurting and finding it hard to see beyond the present crisis. I simply wanted relief, but I knew He was doing more.

As with anyone carrying a burden, the waiting and wondering, the grieving, and the temptation to doubt, can be almost overwhelming. Whether it is for ourselves or a loved one, a physical ailment, or a wound of the soul, our pain can easily disorient us and rob us of our faith.

The words He spoke to me were so simple, and yet it made me stop and think. Had I lost my perspective? Was I getting lost in the pain or looking to a future outcome of victory? Immediately, He reminded me of a truth I had learned just a few days earlier about the robe of righteousness mentioned in Scripture. This robe is not just a symbolic mantle or garment we wear as a sign of our salvation.

This robe holds power and authority.

The fact is, He is the one who gives His sons and daughters this robe because He wore it first.

In the year that King Uzziah died I saw the Lord sitting upon a throne, high and lifted up; and the train of His robe filled the temple.
Isaiah 6:1-2

81

Do you know why the "…train of His robe filled the temple"? I learned that in ancient times when a king had won a great victory and defeated an enemy, the king would walk through the battle ground and take the spoils for his men. But, the greatest recognition for the king that he had been victorious was signified when he would have a piece of the defeated king's robe cut off and then sewn onto the bottom or the train of his own robe. For a king in Old Testament times, the length of his robe (or the train) would, therefore, be a sign or an indication of his greatness. The longer his train, the more victories he had won and the more kings he had defeated.

Think of it! That robe that Christ wears fills the temple because it is so long! It is filled with all His victories sewn onto it. It is not just a symbol of royalty or majesty.

It is a robe that signifies absolute victory over every foe and enemy of our soul!

He has already won every battle we face and conquered every sin, sickness, disease, temptation, weakness, iniquity, and curse. When we enthrone Him as King and worship Him, there is no room left for defeat – only victory. But, it gets better!

I will greatly rejoice in the Lord; my soul shall exult in my God,
for He has clothed me with the garments of salvation;
He has covered me with the robe of righteousness,
as a bridegroom decks himself like a priest with a beautiful head-
dress, and as a bride adorns herself with her jewels.
Isaiah 61:10

He has now put that robe on us! All the victories that He has won are sewn onto that robe and placed on us. He has "mantled" us with victory! We don't have to battle for it. He has already won it for us.

All we have to do is wear it with the confident assurance of its power and authority.

The Lord also showed me that in addition to the victories He has won, each of us have won victories that make that robe even longer. Think of your past victories. Whenever you overcame a sin, a weakness, or temptation, it was marked as a victory for you and your robe got longer. Every time you defeated a particular foe, your robe got longer. Every time you said "No" to the Accuser and "Yes" to God, your robe got longer. Every time you overcame a sin or stronghold, your robe got longer. Your own journey has been marked by victories both large and small and the patches of robe from all those defeated "kings" have been added to your robe.

The enemy, however, does not want you to remember what you've already won. He will do all he can to make the present pain greater than your memory. This is why we need to recall our past victories and remember what the Lord has already done.

I shall not die, but I shall live, and recount the deeds of the Lord!
Psalm 118:17

Look back and consider all the ways in which you have already overcome. Remember the wildernesses you have already come through, the battles you've already won, the lessons learned, and wisdom gained. Don't let the enemy steal your history and don't let your pain in the present become greater than your victory.

The victory is greater than the pain. Remember His finished work and look at this present battle as another patch for your robe. It's already longer than you think.

Thank You, Lord Jesus, for conquering Death and every other foe and enemy of my soul! Thank You that the train of Your robe fills Your temple because of the ultimate victory over sin and death. Thank You for giving me that same victory over every area of my life. I apply Your blood to my life, acknowledging its power to cleanse, heal, and restore me so that I, too, can walk in the righteousness of Christ.

I thank You that any present pain in my own life is nothing compared to the victories already won and the victories to come. I believe that You have given me everything I need to overcome life's challenges and setbacks. Grant me the same joy that You had when facing the cross, so that I might see the glory ahead. I declare that the victory is greater than the pain! For Your sake and glory, Jesus, amen.

ACCESSING
GOD'S GRACE

C an we miss God's grace? Can we be disqualified from or ineligible for the grace of God in walking out our call and destiny?

God's grace is unmerited, and we cannot earn it. Yet, Scripture tells us that we can miss it if we are carrying a chip on our shoulder from the past. Our access to His grace could be hindered if we have allowed any bitterness into our hearts and lives.

> *See to it that no one fails to obtain the grace of God; that no*
> *"root of bitterness" springs up and causes trouble,*
> *and by it many become defiled.*
> *Hebrews 12:15*

This exhortation comes in the middle of a reminder about Esau and how he sold his birthright to his brother for a bowl of soup. His own impatience and greed caused him to trade in the promise of God for a quick fix to his hunger. As a result, when it came time to look for his inheritance, he couldn't find it because he had become embittered towards his brother.

He missed God's grace because of a bitter soul.

There is a grace upon each one of us that enables and empowers us to fulfill our call. If we don't take care of our offenses or any unforgiveness towards others, we will not have access to that grace. I believe this is where deception takes root. Our offenses poison our perspective and we miss the best of what God intends.

That's what happened to Esau. "For you know that afterward, when he desired to inherit the blessing, he was rejected, for he found no chance to repent, though he sought it with tears" (v.17).

This is the sad and destructive nature of bitterness. It blinds us, not only to truth, but to our own sin and responsibility. Even worse, Scripture says that bitterness defiles us. The word defilement means "to taint, stain, pollute, or contaminate." It colors our vision so that everything we see and experience is filtered through our bitterness. This is why it is so deceptive and so dangerous.

Until we repent of our own pride and blame-shifting, we cannot enter into the promised grace God has for us. Though we cannot earn it, we can be locked out of it due to the state of our hearts. Even if we plead with God, as Esau did, we cannot access His grace until we repent and extend forgiveness.

Personally, I need all the help I can get! I have determined to live my life "offense-free." It means that I cannot afford to be bitter towards anyone or hold a grudge. It means I have determined to deal with offenses quickly and thoroughly.

If there is any bitterness in your life, it's not worth it. You are only hurting yourself and cutting off the flow of God's grace into your life. Extending forgiveness is not letting another person off the hook for any wrong doing. It simply frees you from the hold of bitterness.

Choose to repent of any offense you have taken and release those you are holding captive in your heart and mind. Invite God's presence to cleanse your heart and replace your disappointment and pain with His grace. You have tremendous access to God's grace. As you walk free of offense and bitterness, you will experience more and more of His grace to empower you and enable you to see your amazing future with Him.

Father, I choose to live an "offense-free" life. I repent for any bitterness in my life. (Take a moment to name any person you need to forgive. Lay out your case before the Lord, but then leave it with Him.)

Forgive me for holding on to this bitterness, disappointment, and pain. Come and cleanse my heart and mind from these past memories and cover them with Your blood. Change my heart towards love and compassion and remove the defilement from my life. Enable me to see what You see and to love as You love. Renew my mind and empower me by Your Spirit to not hold any grudges but live in freedom and the power of Your grace. In Jesus' name, amen.

It's My Word That Performs, Not You

We all struggle with extremely full schedules and a clutter of "good" things that pile up. The ability to focus and gain steam in numerous areas at the same time can be a challenge. We know the value of operating out of an overflow instead of a deficit. The desire to connect deeply with the Lord is still there, but amidst the busyness, it can be harder to concentrate because of the underlying pressure to "perform."

Out of our desire to make a difference in the world and our need for significance, we can easily get caught in a trap without realizing it. We begin to wonder if we're doing things right – if we're making a difference. We start to compare ourselves with one another and always fall short. Our compulsion to keep up can drain us of our grace and peace of mind.

I asked the Lord how I could manage everything and be a better steward of what He has given me. The first thing He said was to stop and listen:

"I am working in and through you, not because of your performance but because of My covenant. I have called you and set you apart for My purposes. I will be faithful to that. Even when you are distracted or get sidetracked, My purposes still stand because I have spoken My Word and it shall come to pass. Stop looking at how you perform. I am not grading you. Simply do that which I have spoken and be faithful to complete what you started. I will use you for My glory because of My covenant promise, not because of your performance.

It is My Word that is performing, not you '…for I am watching over My word to perform it'" (Jeremiah 1:12).

Our success is due to His working in us, not in our working for Him.

The Prophet of all prophets has spoken His Word over us and He is passionate about seeing that Word fulfilled. When we try to make things happen or start getting ahead of His Word, we only find confusion, chaos, and restlessness. In our efforts to perform better, we can get outside of His grace.

As a trained musician, my understanding of performance is deeply engrained. It always starts with good intentions of "doing my best" and yet so easily turns into a competition, not only with others, but with myself. The Religious Spirit gets attached to it, and before you know it, I'm competing with myself to achieve a self-imposed standard that will be impossible to reach.

There's a difference between obedience and performance.

Obedience is simply doing that which He has told us to say or do. Performance is going beyond what He has spoken in order to get something we think we need or deserve. The lie is that if we "do more", He will "do more." We have bought into an ungodly belief that says the harder we work and the more we produce, the further and higher we will go. However, in the kingdom, it's not how fast we run or how high we climb, but how obedient we are to His Word.

Our human tendency is to try and keep up with others. However, comparison kills us. It causes us to get in someone else's lane and miss our own unique path and purpose. He has called you and has already spoken His Word over you. From the time you said "Yes" to Him, He made a covenant promise to fulfill His purposes in you and finish what He started. It's not up to you to make anything happen. You are not performing for anyone. You simply need to stay in a place of obedience, rest, and His measured grace for every season. His supernatural grace will bear incredible fruit in your life when you simply let His Word do the work. Even if He tells you to walk when everyone else is running, you will still win the race.

It's His covenant promise to you.

Father, thank You for Your Word over my life. Thank You for Your faithfulness in performing that Word and working in me to fulfill Your purpose. Forgive me for striving to make things happen or go beyond what You have said. I delight in Your Word and yield myself to Your dealings and methods so that Your Word will be fulfilled in me and through me. Thank You for Your covenant promise. I stand secure in it and know that, with Your help, I will win the race that is marked out for me, for Your glory. Amen.

GROWING IN DISCERNMENT

There is a great need for the gift of discernment among believers in this hour. That which is evil is being called good and that which is good is being called evil (Isaiah 5:20). No one knows what or who to believe anymore.

The world judges things by what they see and hear with their natural senses. They determine what is true by what is played on the news or social media, and by what others say. However, we as Spirit-empowered Christ-followers should dig deeper. Discerning between good and evil is not something that comes naturally. It must come from the Spirit of God.

The natural person does not accept the things of the Spirit of God,
for they are folly to him, and he is not able to understand them
because they are spiritually discerned.
1 Corinthians 2:14

How do we grow in discernment? How can we learn to decipher what we hear so as to see the truth more clearly? Here are some keys that will help you grow in your ability to discern what is of God, what is of man, and what is of the devil:

Build a good track record:

But solid food is for the mature,
for those who have their powers of discernment trained by
constant practice to distinguish good from evil.
Hebrews 5:14

Part of growing in discernment is by practice and gaining a personal track record that tells us we're making good calls. Mature discernment only comes through a consistent walk in the truth that bears the fruit of correct judgment. Look at past judgments you've made and learn from your successes as well as your mistakes.

Get accurate information:

An intelligent heart acquires knowledge,
and the ear of the wise seeks knowledge.
Proverbs 18:19

Before making judgments or jumping on any bandwagon, verify the facts. This is critical in the digital age when it's so easy to assume what we read or hear is the whole truth and nothing but the truth. Just as a prophetic word should be tested, so should every sound-bite that we hear. Be willing to search for the truth and ask Holy Spirit to guide you to God's Word for wisdom and revelation.

Gift of discerning of spirits:

I Corinthians 12:7 speaks of the gift or divine enablement to discern the motivation of a person, whether it be of the Holy Spirit, a demonic spirit, or the flesh. This is a supernatural gift that enables us to perceive the true source of information and inspiration. It is an unction of the spirit and should guide our prayers as well as assist us in ministering to any situation needing God's wisdom and power.

Now we have received not the spirit of the world,
but the Spirit who is from God, that we might understand
the things freely given us by God.
1 Corinthians 2:12

Sometimes, our own preconceived ideas or assumptions may limit our perception of truth. If we are to live by the Spirit of truth we need to lay down our personal agenda and listen for His. We must be willing to be directed by God's Spirit and then adjust to what He reveals to us, even when it means changing our own perceptions and beliefs.

Every believer is called to discernment. It takes practice and an understanding of God's word and God's heart. Learning through the process can teach us how to make right judgments and grow in wisdom.

Holy Spirit, come and teach me to discern rightly according to the Father's heart and Word. Grant me insight in what is true and help me distinguish between good and evil. Clear my mind and current understanding of anything that does not bear truth according to the Word of God. Grant me understanding in things of the Spirit that I might pray more effectively, exercise wise counsel, and bless others for Your glory. Amen.

His Word
is
Like Fire

Let the prophet who has a dream recount the dream, but let the one who has My word speak it faithfully. For what has straw to do with grain? declares the Lord. Is not My word like fire, declares the Lord, and a hammer that breaks a rock in pieces?

Jeremiah 23:28-29

WHAT YOU BELIEVE IS
WHAT YOU WILL BECOME

...be renewed in the spirit of your minds,
and (to) put on the new self, created after the likeness
of God in true righteousness and holiness.
Ephesians 4:24

As powerful as prayer is, our desire to be transformed into His image will not come as a result of how much or how long we pray. Prayer may be a vehicle that addresses various issues in our lives, but it is what we believe about those issues that will determine whether any long-term change happens. The struggles and strongholds we deal with are often a wrestling match with our minds – what and how we think. Our emotions are fed by our thoughts and our faith is fed by what we believe.

What you *feel* is simply the result of something you *believe*.

I went through a season where I felt like other church leaders were looking down on me because I was a woman. Though I knew there were theological and doctrinal beliefs that supported my feelings, I realized that my perspective might be limited. I also knew I had a choice in how I responded.

As I went to prayer and acknowledged my negative feelings, the Lord showed me that I had been feeling like a victim – because I *thought* like one. I had begun to believe that I was a victim of gender discrimination. A victim of the Religious spirit. A victim of traditions of man. This resulted in feelings of discouragement and defeat and automatically defending myself at every turn.

I repented of my mindsets, knowing that this was not how God saw me. He revealed His heart and truth for me as His daughter and I settled in my own heart who and Whose I was, apart from what man said or did. No longer did I need to apologize or defend myself. I simply stood on the truth and let Him validate who I was and what I was called to do. Once I changed my thinking, my feelings changed as my reactions and responses adjusted to the new-found truth.

Determining the source of our feelings, both good and bad, will reveal what we believe. The devil is the father of lies and the only hold he will have over us is if we believe a lie. He will have access to our lives and wreak havoc with our emotions if we feel something that is based on a lie. However, God's truth can displace those lies and set us free.

If you are dealing with a stronghold or being tormented by negative feelings, praying "against" it is incomplete. Ask the Lord what you are thinking about that situation and compare it with His Word. When you recognize what the ungodly belief is, you can then ask God to reveal His truth to displace the lie. Many times, we fight needless battles against the devil when all that is needed is a reality-check with what is true. Don't get stuck in past mindsets formed through disappointments or failures. Renew your mind and start thinking like God. The more you believe like Him, the more you will become like Him.

Father, I ask that You would reveal any lies that I am believing that are warring against my mind and flesh (Romans 7:23). Help me to see what I believe in the light of Your truth and Your Word. I ask for the mind of Christ to come and cleanse my thoughts so that I would be renewed in my thinking and transformed in my perspectives. May I walk in the truth and the light, and become more and more like Your son, Jesus, for Whose sake I live. Amen.

The Outrageous Possibilities of Prayer

In John 14-16, Jesus is giving His farewell speech to His disciples. In His last few remaining hours on earth, He is reminding them of the most critical truths that He has taught them. He wants to make sure they remember what He has said so that they will walk in the kingdom realities He so powerfully demonstrated while with them.

It is notable that in the space of just three chapters, He says five different times, in seven different verses, "If you remain in Me and My words remain in you, ask whatever you wish and it will be done for you" (John 14:13-14, 15:7-8, 16, 16:23-24). This is not to evaluate what we ask for, but to consider the outrageous possibilities in prayer!

He specifically states that the Father will give them whatever they "wish" for. That word means "to desire, to love, to take delight in, have pleasure." His excitement is almost palpable throughout His message as He repeats this admonition over and over, hoping they get just how much His Father loves to answer their requests!

Obviously, there is context. Surrounding these verses is the principle of abiding in the Vine. There is an underlying assumption that our hearts are so closely knit to and aligned with the Heavenly Father, that His wishes, His desires, and His longings, have now become ours. It is this kind of relationship that brings oneness of heart, unity of purpose, and power in prayer.

When we are truly one with the Father, answered prayer will be the result.

Consider the prayers you have prayed and the things you have requested of the Lord. Are they being answered? If not, go back to Him and ask if there is anything amiss in your relationship with Him. He truly desires to answer your prayers and He loves to bless His sons and daughters. Ultimately, He wants to be one with you and He wants you to think like Him!

As you consider this reality in your own life, determine to walk in this kind of abiding relationship that joins your heart, mind, and will to the Father's. Dare to ask Him what He places on your heart and expect to see results. It brings Him joy and He gets all the glory.

Heavenly Father, I want to abide in You, cling to Your Word, and live from Your presence. May Your desires become my desires. May Your thoughts become my thoughts, and may Your will become my will. I thank You that as I abide in You, I can ask for the very things You place on my heart so that all the world will know of Your goodness. Thank You for making me a conduit of Your blessings from heaven to earth through my witness and my prayers. In Jesus' name, amen.

You Are That Platform

As believers and children of God, we have the incredible opportunity to not only hear the Father's voice, but to be an oracle of His grace. Through our voices, we can speak of the Lord's goodness and the Father's plans that will bring hope and a future to His people. We become conduits of His voice as we share the things that are on His heart and mind.

However, we have an Adversary who wants to shut us up! He does not want the Father's voice to be heard. Nor does he want us to speak it. He knows the power we have been given and he is jealous of our intimacy with the Father and the great favor He has given us to speak from His throne.

I will also speak of Your testimonies before kings
and shall not be put to shame.
Psalm 119:46

You have a voice and the Father wants you to use that voice to declare His goodness to those around you. Do not let the enemy try and shut you down from speaking what is true and good. Do not let fear and condemnation cause you to cower in the corner. Do not disqualify yourself because your voice is quiet or seemingly weak in the world's eyes.

Know that when He speaks to you and through you, your voice carries weight in the spirit. Know that when you join with just one other believer, your agreement has power. When your voice agrees with His, it has power in the spirit to displace strongholds and set captives free!

There are some of you who think you need a platform in order to speak. But, the Lord says to you,

"You do not need a platform for YOU ARE that platform"!

You carry the words of life and when you speak a true word from heaven, the weight and authority of the Father will push through those gates that have been closed and the King of Glory will make His entrance. What the enemy has tried to stop, your voice can move!

On that day your mouth will be opened to the fugitive, and you shall speak and be no longer mute. So, you will be a sign to them, and they will know that I am the Lord.
Ezekiel 24:27

You are a carrier and dispenser of truth and justice, freedom and hope. When you speak His heart, all of heaven backs you up and atmospheres change. Begin to lift your voice and praise Him. Even as you speak God's praises, the enemy will be silenced as your voice displaces his lies. Your voice is powerful. Use it.

I will bless the Lord at all times!
His praise shall continually be in my mouth!
My soul makes its boast in the Lord; let the humble hear and be glad. Oh, magnify the Lord with me, and let us exalt His name together! I sought the Lord, and He answered me and delivered me from all my fears.
Psalm 34:1-4

Rise Up, David, and Speak to That Giant

It is God's joy and pleasure to use those who appear weak and limited in order to annihilate the proud and the haughty. Do not *underestimate* the authority of heaven. Do not *overestimate* the power of the enemy. Do not *underestimate* the God of all glory that resides in *you!*

Many believers are being called onto the frontlines of our culture to speak up and take a stand against the voices that seek to drown out the victory that is rightfully ours. The Lord is calling upon the Davids of this hour to rise up with courage and boldness and speak to the spiritual giants that have come against our faith, our identity, and our inheritance.

Many of these modern-day Davids are women and children. Some are disillusioned "has-beens" whom the Lord is calling back into active service. Others are "nobodies" from man's perspective. However, it is not a matter of age, position, or reputation. It is a matter of divine calling and preparation by heaven in the hidden place that has qualified those who are being used in this hour to defeat strongholds and principalities.

Are *you* one of them?

It is time to call out these Davids and recognize the favor of God on them to release and decree their faith and word of hope. Though the Goliaths of this hour are constantly taunting and threatening us through fear and intimidation, the battle can be quickly turned by the obedience of just one David.

Just as David's brothers tried to silence his voice through fear, intimidation, and empty threats, those who have been called in this hour must take courage and appeal to the King. It is our King of Glory who will release these warriors of valor, not because of man's commendation, but because of their faith and boldness. It is those who have been ministering to the Lord in the secret place that will rise up and be mantled with greater authority to defeat greater giants in the land.

Has the Lord been preparing you in the hidden place? Is there a giant He is preparing you to face?

- It will require a sensitive ear to hear the Father's invitation to the battlefield.
- It will require an obedient heart to look past the limitations and seeming weaknesses of the flesh.
- It will require a Kingdom perspective to overlook distractions and comparisons that would seek to disqualify participation.
- It will require boldness and determination to step out in faith.

To the Davids of this hour the Lord would say:

"Stop listening to your accusers! Don't listen to the voices that tell you you're too young, too old, not trained, not ready! I am the One who has called you and I am the One who will anoint you! I have prepared you for this hour and I will back you up! GO and declare My Kingdom. Stand before the giant and let your voice be heard. I will speak through you and will shatter the lies with My truth and My presence. Be a carrier of My glory and release your faith and your prayers to take down the giants in the land"!

It was not David's stone that ultimately killed Goliath, but a sword (I Samuel 17:51). The prayers released in faith may take the enemy to the ground, but it is the Word of the Lord that will overcome, defeat, and decapitate the enemy!

103

Though the battle may be turned through our prayers, it is the word of our testimony that will establish the rightful heir.

David said to the Philistine, "You come against me with sword and spear and javelin, but I come against you in the name of the LORD Almighty, the God of the armies of Israel, whom you have defied. This day the LORD will hand you over to me, and I'll strike you down and cut off your head.
1 Samuel 17:45-47

"Rise up, David! Rise up and open your mouth, for you are the rightful heir in this land. Open your mouth and do not be silent. Let the cries of heaven come through you to a people of desperation, fear, and unbelief. Do not disqualify yourself but follow heaven's lead and stand before the giants. Release your prayers and then testify to My goodness and My presence in this land. Let the world know that I am the God who saves; I am the God who delivers, and I am the God of victory!"

It is God's joy and pleasure to use those who appear weak and limited in order to annihilate the proud and the haughty. Do not *underestimate* the authority of heaven. Do not *overestimate* the power of the enemy. Do not *underestimate* the God of all glory that resides in you!

Heavenly Father, thank You for preparing me to be a David to stand up and speak Your Word against the spiritual giants that defy Your holy Name. Grant me the courage to face the giants and boldly declare Your truth. Bless all those who have been called as Davids in this hour to take a stand for the sake of Your kingdom. For Jesus' sake, amen.

They Must Come Together
or not at All

In a dream, I saw a group of people praying in the corner, huddled together in earnest intercession. Before them in the far distance was a mountain. I knew it represented kingdom authority and heaven's council. The intercessors were seeking to connect to this mountain, to align themselves in order to break through the veil and bring heaven's authority to bear on the earth. Yet, the connection was not clear. Interaction with this mountain was blocked.

Knowing we were not fully aligned, I stepped out of the group and began to move to the left, holding an invisible kind of line connected to this mountain. I knew we had to come into perfect alignment in order to break through. Finally, after continuing to move little by little to the left, watching this line of communication eventually settle into place, I waited.

After a few moments I saw something begin to move in the distance. Slowly, but steadily, I saw three distinct Beings emerge from the heart of the mountain. Closer and closer they came until I saw what they were. Three large eagles, stately, bearing immense authority and grace. As they drew closer I knew they had been summoned. I also knew they were looking at me.

As they drew closer, a fear and dread began to come over me at the authority and power I sensed coming from them. They were deliberate, forceful, yet moving cautiously…looking…listening. At last, the three huge figures hovered immediately above me, looking down at me with a silent, yet unmistakably loud message:

"We come together, or not at all!"

I woke up feeling the immensity of their presence. It didn't take long to interpret their meaning. This was a message for the Church in this hour. It is the Father, Son, and Holy Spirit speaking to us as we are coming together and interceding for a spiritual revival in the land. Until we acknowledge the fullness of each person of the Godhead, we will not see the fullness of heaven come to the earth.

We cannot pick and choose which expression of the Trinity we prefer. We cannot focus on one at the expense of the other. Each represents and expresses God's heart and character in a different dimension (2 Corinthians 13:14).

- **God,** our Creator and loving heavenly Father.
- **Jesus Christ**, the only Way to salvation through the cross.
- **Holy Spirit**, the full expression and manifestation of the Father's heart.

Every church or denomination tends to focus on one of the aspects of the Trinity more than the others. There are "Grace" churches that tend to focus on the heart of the Father and His unconditional love and acceptance towards all. There are "Word" churches that focus on the Living Word of Jesus Christ and the gospel He preached. There are the "Holy Spirit" churches which embrace the gifts of the Spirit and encourage all to "jump in the river."

Though all of these are expressions of the Godhead, they are incomplete by themselves. Even as believers, if we focus our relationship on just one Person of the Trinity, we will miss out on the fullness of who God is and all that He has for us. The reality is this:

They are ONE.
They cannot be divided.
If we want heaven to come to earth - they must come together.

There is one body and one Spirit, just as you were called to one hope when you were called; one Lord, one faith, one baptism; one God and Father of all, Who is over all and through all and in all.
Ephesians 4:4-6

Heaven has heard our summons for revival and has been moving ever closer. Yet, we must be ready to receive the fullness of the Godhead and how He might come and work among us. Can we align our hearts, thoughts, beliefs, and prayers in order to see the fullness of heaven released?

They are waiting on us.

Heavenly Father, I worship You as Almighty God, the Father of all creation. I give praise to Jesus Christ, my Savior, the true and living Word and only Way to the Father. I honor Holy Spirit and welcome His working in my life to reveal and demonstrate the love and power of the Godhead. Forgive me for any dishonor or neglect I have had towards one Person of the Three-in-One. Help me to walk in the fullness of Who You are so I can reflect all of Your glory, all of Your wonder, and all of Your awe. For Christ's sake, amen.

PURSUING *His* PRESENCE

Seek the Lord and His strength;
seek His presence continually.

Psalm 105:4

GOD'S MANIFEST PRESENCE

And he (Moses) said to Him,
"If Your presence will not go with me, do not bring us up from here."
Exodus 33:15

When we speak of God's "presence" there are three different aspects or distinctions of His presence in Scripture. As we understand these distinctions, we can come to embrace and pursue His manifest presence in a way that enriches and empowers our lives and those around us.

God's omnipresence fills every place at all times.

Can a man hide himself in secret places so that I cannot see him? declares the Lord. Do I not fill heaven and earth? declares the Lord.
Jeremiah 23:24

God's omnipresence is always with us. We may not think about it or "feel" it, yet He is there. The Hebrew word most often used for "presence" means God's "face." He is not some impersonal force, but a Father who is always watching over us, closer than we realize.

God's indwelling presence empowers believers to walk in the Spirit.

And I will put My Spirit within you, and cause you to walk in My statutes and be careful to obey My rules.
Ezekiel 36:27

Do you not know that you are God's temple
and that God's Spirit dwells in you?
1 Corinthians 3:16

When we receive Jesus as Lord, we get a package deal – Father, Son, and Holy Spirit. The Holy Spirit dwells in us as believers and empowers us to be who we were created to be, and do what we were created to do. The indwelling Spirit gives us the power to live a godly life and demonstrate the kingdom here on earth.

God's manifest presence is the tangible reality and evidence of God's presence and power. It is specific and directed.

When the day of Pentecost arrived, they were all together in one place. And suddenly there came from heaven a sound like a mighty rushing wind, and it filled the entire house where they were sitting.
Acts 2:1-2

God came and met His people in a powerful demonstration of His presence that built their faith and empowered their witness. They went out radically transformed due to the tangible evidence of God's Spirit they had experienced.

We can count on God's **omnipresence** to be with us at all times regardless of any initiative on our part. His **indwelling** presence will be seen through the fruit of our lives as we yield ourselves to Him in obedience.

His **manifest** presence, however, is demonstrated in order to display Himself to others. He parted the Red Sea; He revealed Himself in a cloud and pillar of fire to lead His people through the wilderness; He descended as a dove upon Jesus at His baptism to announce His pleasure.

Whenever God comes in a tangible way that is seen or felt, it stirs hearts, builds faith, and gives glory to the One Who alone holds all power in His hands. We do not need to fear this tangible evidence of God's presence because it shows His heart to be real and personal.

I have experienced God's manifest presence in many different ways. It first started in the secret place as I would press into His heart. Most of the time it was unexpected. It would come in the form of a blanket of peace or a burning fire in my heart. Other times my whole body would shake under the power of His presence and love. Regardless of how it felt, I always knew that He had drawn closer. It let me know that He was at work and was responding to my heart-cry.

I have also experienced His manifest presence corporately during worship or at times when a small group of us have simply waited on Him together. In each case, it came at a time when we were in total oneness of heart and attitude. It was as if our hearts became so fused together in unity that we opened a portal in the spirit through which His Spirit came down. When this happens, everyone in the room can tell something has changed. You can *feel* the difference.

I believe this is what happened in the Old Testament when the cloud of God's glory came into the Temple.

And when the priests came out of the Holy Place (for all the priests who were present had consecrated themselves, without regard to their divisions) ...the house of the Lord was filled with a cloud, so that the priests could not stand to minister because of the cloud, for the glory of the Lord filled the house of God.
2 Chronicles 5:11-14

God is here whether we see Him or not. We know this by faith. And yet, as the days grow darker and evil increases, it is His desire to show Himself and reveal Himself through His people. He wants to demonstrate to the world that He is, indeed, God and is holy and powerful. What happened at Pentecost was just a deposit of more to come.

Now the One who has fashioned us for this very purpose is God,
Who has given us the Spirit as a deposit,
guaranteeing what is to come.
2 Corinthians 5:5 NIV

We do not pursue God's tangible presence simply for a personal experience. We pursue it so that others can see Him and know Him. The Church was born as a result of His manifest presence coming and empowering His people. We should expect no less today.

Lord, I hunger for a greater measure of Your presence in my life. Stir my heart and draw me deeper into the secret place where I can meet with You. Thank You for Your indwelling presence that is with me. Fill me afresh that I might know You more and bear more fruit for Your glory. Pull me closer to Your heart so that I might be united with You and fully abide in Your presence. Teach me to wait on You and watch for You. I give You full control of how You might show Yourself to me. May our times together result in revealing Your love and goodness to those around me and may I shine forth Your glory. For Christ's sake, amen.

What Happens
in His Presence?

The goal of practicing His presence on a consistent basis is to have an exchange. We exchange our stress, our preoccupations, our anxieties, and all that we carry as human beings for His peace, His promise, and His purpose. It is a transaction of the spirit where we come out different than how we went in. Here is what we can expect to happen when we make this exchange:

We exchange our stress for His rest.

The LORD replied (to the nation of Israel),
"My Presence will go with you, and I will give you rest."
Exodus 33:14

We cannot hear from God when we are stressed or overworked. Even the world knows that quiet meditation is good for the soul. Unless we give our minds and bodies opportunities to be still, we will soon grow tired and weary. He wants us to live from a place of rest. That's when we can have clear minds and a right perspective.

The enemy is silenced.

In the shelter of Your presence You hide them from the intrigues of men; in Your dwelling You keep them safe from accusing tongues.
Psalm 31:20

What an amazing promise that when we come into this place under the shadow of His wings, He hides us from our Accuser! Think about it. The devil is not going to go where God's presence is. He will virtually run from it. The place of God's presence is a guaranteed spiritual bunker where you can get away from any enemy interference to become anchored and secured in His grace.

We receive blessings, joy, and an unshakable faith.

Surely You have granted him eternal blessings and made him glad with the joy of Your presence. For the king trusts in the LORD; through the unfailing love of the Most High he will not be shaken.
Psalm 21:6-7

This says that being in God's presence will give us joy. Gladness instead of sorrow; joy instead of mourning; laughter instead of gloom! That's a great exchange rate! When we walk in the joy of the Lord, we are stronger. His presence empowers us to stand secure and not be shaken by life's tests and trials.

His presence will overflow to those around us.

When Moses came down from Mount Sinai...(he) did not know that the skin of his face shone because he had been talking with God.
Exodus 34:29

This is the grace of the Lord and nothing we can accomplish on our own. Moses had no idea what he looked like when he came off that mountain with God. His face simply reflected what he had just beheld. This is the promise and the purpose of spending time in God's presence. We will reflect His glory and come out looking like Him. It can change everything around us, without even trying.

We receive an increase of the Holy Spirit's empowering gifts.

When the day of Pentecost came, they were all together in one place.
Acts 2:1

On this day, the believers were simply spending time in God's presence – waiting and watching. They had no idea what was about to happen, but the exchange they got literally changed the world.

Father, I want to experience the realities of Your presence so that I can exchange my human frailties for Your tangible presence. Teach me to wait on You and give myself wholly to Your Spirit that I might be transformed. I receive Your rest. I thank You for silencing the voice of my Accuser and for the joy I receive as I fix my gaze on You. Enable me to take this time to be still, to know that You alone are my life source for today. I love Your presence, God! In Jesus' name, amen.

Keys to Entering His Presence

What are the factors that help usher in God's Presence? Do we have any role in seeing His manifest presence come and move? We certainly can't force God's presence to come, nor should we try to make something happen. His call to us is to simply prepare the way through posturing our hearts rightly.

We are not seeking an experience to feel something.
We are pursuing His face to be transformed.

Here are a few keys in helping you to posture your own heart to make room for His presence:

Quiet your soul.

O Lord, my heart is not lifted up; my eyes are not raised too high;
I do not occupy myself with things too great
and too marvelous for me.
But I have calmed and quieted my soul, like a weaned child with
its mother; like a weaned child is my soul within me.
Psalm 131:1-2

Determine to clear the clutter in your heart and mind. As you come to Him, put on quiet instrumental music or simply enjoy the silence to help you relax and focus on His presence. Determine to make the time about relationship, not agenda. If nothing else happens, simply let Him have center stage for a while and get some rest!

Get real.

*Whenever Moses went in before the Lord to speak with Him, he
would remove the veil, until he came out.*
Exodus 34:34a

If we truly want to be one with Him, we have to remove the mask,
the pretense, and the fear of being known. That which separates us
from connecting with the Lord is often because we, ourselves, put up
barriers. Emotionally and mentally we can put up defenses that keep
Him from drawing closer. Determine to remove your emotional veil
and get real. He won't shun you. He will welcome you as you simply
share with Him what He already knows.

Keep a clear conscience.

*But You have upheld me because of my integrity,
and set me in Your presence forever.*
Psalms 41:12

The word for "integrity" means "uprightness and innocence." Our
integrity is measured by how truthful we are and how we walk before
others. It opens the way for God's presence to move in unhindered.
If He brings anything to mind that is clogging your conscience, clear
it out!

Become wholly His.

*May He strengthen your hearts so that you will be blameless
and holy in the presence of our God and Father when our
Lord Jesus comes with all His holy ones.*
1 Thessalonians 3:13

As we are *holy*, we become *wholly* His. It is this place of purity of heart that His presence can come the strongest. This is where He dwells. In heavenly places, the angelic beings are right at His feet in the presence of His holiness. This is the place where He dwells and puts His feet up!

Thus says the Lord: "Heaven is My throne, and the earth is My footstool; what is the house that you would build for Me, and what is the place of My rest?"
Isaiah 66:1

Heavenly Father, I want to be a resting place for Your presence! Teach me to draw near to You with clean hands and a pure heart and to continually seek Your face. Strengthen my heart so that I will be blameless and holy in Your sight. Set me in Your presence, today. Teach me to rest and quiet my soul so that I can know You more. Thank You for revealing Yourself through Your manifest presence so that I may show forth Your glory in increasing manner. To You alone belongs all the glory, amen.

HE IS PASSIONATE
ABOUT US

Just before I wake up, I'm seeing Him struggle to come back from the other side of a great chasm. He is clinging to the edge as He has come from seeing "Her" and is deeply distressed because of His love for Her. Though He desperately wanted to stay He couldn't. Not yet. He longs for the time when He can be with Her, but She is not ready. His very essence is too powerful for Her. His nature would overwhelm Her. His heart aches for Her, but the atmosphere must change.

When I awoke from this dream, I felt the passion of the Lord's heart. I knew He wanted me to know the great love He has for His Bride. He longs to be with us in tangible ways. He always has. His heart aches for us and He wants to come in greater measure to reveal His presence and power.

Our spiritual Adversary would like us to think that God is, somehow, holding out on us because He is displeased with us. We can fall into a trap of doubting God's love for us simply because we haven't seen the fullness of His promise, yet. The fact is, He heard our cries for help long ago. He proved His love over 2000 years ago when He came as a man to take our sins on Himself. It was in His first "coming" that the fullness of His love was expressed on the cross. The powerful manifestation of His love was already demonstrated on the earth when He died and rose again.

There is no further need for Him to prove His love for you and me!

However, as we face the increasing spiritual darkness overtaking everything around us, we are again at heaven's mercy. Both personally and corporately, we are in desperate need of a Savior and Redeemer! We need His tangible, manifest presence now more than ever.

We aren't just looking for a *visitation*, but a *habitation* of His presence. Though He is certainly "with us" through His omnipresence, He desires to come even closer in ways that are undeniable and supernatural. He wants the entire world to see and know Him like never before in all His glory. Yet, even as many are praying for revival and spiritual awakening on the earth, we can't assume this will happen just because we pray more or get more passionate in our pursuit. We must make ourselves ready.

Let us rejoice and exult and give Him the glory, for the marriage of the Lamb has come, and His Bride has made herself ready.
Revelation 19:7

We are not waiting on Him. He is waiting on us.

The Lord dwells on high in heaven's atmosphere where His glory and goodness are abundant. His holiness saturates that realm and it is the very air He breathes. That is why, in my dream, He seemed to be short of breath when coming back from the earth. He was illustrating how important it is for us to continue to pursue His holiness and His manifest presence in our lives, for it is the atmosphere of heaven that will draw Him back.

As you grow in the awareness of God's presence in your own life, consider the atmosphere you live in. Are you attracting His presence in your daily walk? Are you clearing your heart of anything that would hinder the fullness and power of the Holy Spirit? Are you reflecting the same qualities of heaven that would draw Him closer?

Your Bridegroom is passionate for you! He longs to show Himself strong on your behalf and pour out His goodness on you! He is not holding out on you. He is praying for you and asking the Father to sanctify your heart and purify your life so that you can walk in the fullness of His presence.

Determine to carry the aroma of Christ and atmosphere of heaven wherever you go. Through your words and actions, create a place for Him to come and manifest Himself in you and through you so that others will be changed and transformed by the power of His love.

Lord Jesus, I thank You for Your love for me that has never waned. I thank You for reminding me how passionate You are to be with me and show Yourself strong on my behalf. Help me to be all that You have intended so that we can truly be one. Teach me to walk in Your ways and make You the Love of my life. May I become more aware of the atmosphere of heaven so that through my words and actions, Your presence will permeate everything I say and do. For Your glory and honor, Jesus. Amen.

SHIFTING TO A PRESENCE REALITY

We must shift from a warfare mentality to a presence reality. Spiritual warfare may be necessary for a season, but it was never intended to be a lifestyle. We were created to live from and in God's presence.

You make known to me the path of life; in Your presence there is fullness of joy; at Your right hand are pleasures forevermore.
Psalm 16:11

In my early years as an intercessor, I thought it was part of my call to battle things out in the spirit to be effective. I was led to believe that the intensity of the spiritual battle could be an indication of the importance of the assignment. Therefore, I began to take subtle pride in the fact that I was such a persistent and dedicated prayer warrior for the Lord. The problem was, I was easily tired and didn't see many results. I sometimes felt like the battle was never won. What I had worn as a badge of honor, soon became a yoke of oppression. That's when the Lord showed me a different approach.

I began to understand the power of God's manifest presence.

I started to research the Scripture and saw that throughout biblical history, the greatest victories came because of God's tangible presence, not because of man's skills at warfare:

- The power of praise tore down the walls at Jericho (Joshua 6)
- Jehoshaphat's army of worshipers routed the enemy (2 Chronicles 20)

- The wind of His presence created a road in the Red Sea (Exodus 14:21-22).

Even in the New Testament, the followers of Christ were more focused on winning souls to the kingdom than they were in fighting the devil. The biblical pattern for victory was rarely focused on warfare tactics as much as the reality of God's presence.

Praying with this understanding reminds us of just how powerful God's presence is to annihilate every spiritual enemy we face. As we fix our thoughts and attitudes on His presence we are no longer under the weight of the battle, but lifted up in His peace.

Though the mountains be shaken and the hills be removed,
yet My unfailing love for you will not be shaken nor My covenant
of peace be removed, says the Lord, Who has compassion on you.
Isaiah 54:10

Some believers may become preoccupied with spiritual warfare and unnecessarily fight and engage the enemy. Though there are strategic times to do this, it shouldn't be the norm. We often give the enemy far too much attention by continually focusing on what he is doing instead of what God is doing. If we truly believe that God has already won the victory, it is from this place and perspective that we should stand. We must remember the power of His presence to displace and disarm the enemy simply by standing on His word and promise.

There is no glory in battle. Our glory should be in The One who has already defeated the devil. Perhaps if we spent more time in celebration of His victory, we wouldn't be so tempted to fight an enemy that's already lost.

Father, Thank You for the victory that has already been won! Forgive me for giving too much attention to what the enemy is doing instead of what You have already done. I rejoice in Your presence to defeat and annihilate my enemies. I stand in the power of Your presence to displace the darkness and bring light and truth into my life. For Yours is the Kingdom, now and forever! Amen.

God's Glory and the Fear of the Lord

I had never had an open vision before (not in my "mind's eye, but with my eyes open). But, now I had one – in a dream.

I was walking on a road with many people, all going in the same direction. All the sudden behind my right shoulder, a huge golden beam of light from the heavens shone down and began to move across the sky in front of me from right to left. It was massive, and it was evident it was not man-made. It began to engulf everything it touched.

At the same time, I looked up to my right and in the sky was a huge screen. On it I saw a map of the world. It was as if I was seeing and experiencing this phenomenon from two different dimensions. I saw this all-encompassing light start at the eastern part of the map near Australia and it began to slowly move west across the entire globe.

The light filled the entire sky and was full of glory and power. It seemed to move across the center of the map, touching different countries in varying degrees. I knew that what I was seeing and experiencing was global and affecting everyone everywhere.

I heard myself shouting "It's happening! It's happening!" and my heart began to race with excitement. This light was multi-dimensional. It not only went across the surface of the earth, but went underneath in varying degrees of color and richness. The deeper it penetrated, the deeper its color and impact. It was powerful, distinct, and moved with great authority.

I was immediately overwhelmed with joy and awe and fell to my knees as I realized the immensity of what was happening. I cried out, "It's a sign! Get ready!"

I knew it was His glory covering the earth.

Yet, I could sense the fear around me, the uncertainty of what was taking place. As people looked up, dazed, and in shock of what was taking place, I shouted out without hesitation, "It's coming! Yes! But, for those who believe…it's going to be awesome!" I knew there would be those who would not be ready and great fear would seize them. The fear of the Lord was coming in great glory and power and everything in its path was going to be affected. Even so, what was happening was real and it was glorious.

In this vision, I knew I was seeing God's glory begin to cover the earth and it carried with it the fear of the Lord. For those whose hearts were aligned to His, it was glorious and resulted in awe and worship. But, for those whose hearts were divided and set against Him, it brought dread and terror.

When the people saw the thunder and lightning and heard the trumpet and saw the mountain in smoke, they trembled with fear. They stayed at a distance and said to Moses, "Speak to us yourself and we will listen. But do not have God speak to us or we will die." Moses said to the people, "Do not be afraid. God has come to test you, so that the fear of God will be with you to keep you from sinning." Exodus 20:18-20

The Lord was sending a message to be prepared for this coming glory.

The fear of the Lord is necessary in bringing the sons and daughters to the Father. It is meant to keep our hearts pure and holy before Him in order to receive our full inheritance and blessing. It is not sent for punishment or subjection, but for our good, our prosperity, and our joy. It is not something to avoid, but to embrace.

Who, then, are those who fear the Lord? He will instruct them in the ways they should choose. They will spend their days in prosperity, and their descendants will inherit the land. The Lord confides in those who fear Him; He makes His covenant known to them.
Psalm 25:12-14

The Father wants to reveal His fullness to us. He wants for us to know His goodness as well as His glory. But it is extremely powerful. Our flesh cannot handle His glory! And yet, this is what the fear of the Lord does. It helps shape and mold a heart that is rightly postured so that we can receive all that He intends to pour out upon our lives. His glory will transform us from the inside out. As we come to know the power of His love, we will not fear Him, but learn to welcome His holiness and power, for therein lies the kingdom.

"The remarkable thing about God is that when you fear God, you fear nothing else, whereas if you do not fear God, you fear everything else." (Oswald Chambers)

Father, thank You for Your coming glory! I welcome the fear of the Lord in my life so that I might be fully prepared to see You face-to-face without fear. Do Your work in my life so that I might behold Your glory and testify to others of Your goodness. I pray for those who are not ready and ask that You would draw them by Your Spirit to see Your goodness and Your love. Help us to prepare the way for heaven to come to earth so the world can receive You in all Your glory. Amen!

I Save the Best
for Last

Those were the words I heard as God's presence came on me at the end of our weekly prayer time at church. We had already been resting and waiting in God's presence for an hour and I was ready to circle up with closing prayer. But then…unexpectedly…. His prescence came.

This same thing happened a few weeks earlier, as well. The last five minutes of our hourly ritual turned from simply *waiting*, to being *weighted* with His manifest presence. When we were transitioning to finish our time of worship, He came in and began to minister at the very end…at the last. I heard Him say:

> *"For those who will tarry and wait, I will come.*
> *For those who pull on My heart, I save the best for the last!"*

This idea comes from John 2 where Jesus attended the wedding at Cana and turned the water into wine, unexpectedly, when it wasn't expected, and it wasn't time! Jesus himself said it wasn't His time yet (John 2:4). So, what changed His mind?

Someone pulled on His heart and He poured out His best.

It was His own mother that stepped out in faith and decided to override her son – her Lord – and dare to believe that His heart was bigger than His timetable!

Mary had told Jesus that there was no more wine. They had run out after hours of celebration. When she mentioned it to Him, He simply said, "Woman, why do you involve Me? My hour has not yet come" (John 2:4). What appears to be a rebuke is actually quite the opposite. In the Greek, this word "woman" is a term of endearment. He is not rebuking her. He's baiting her! I imagine He even did it with a twinkle in His eye! He was not challenging her understanding; He was challenging her heart. What appeared to be a reminder of some sovereignly divined schedule and order of events, turned out to be an invitation.

He was testing her…just like He's testing us.

What did she really want? What did she really believe? Would she simply acquiesce and quietly sit back in obedience waiting for that "magical moment" when it was "time"? Would she feel guilty for even suggesting the thought?

Or… would she dare herself to believe in everything she had been secretly hiding for years – that He was, indeed, the Son of God and able to do…. anything. How well had she learned to know the power of His love through the years as her son?

I imagine as she looked into His eyes that reflected immense pools of love and affection, she decided to take the bait and step out. In a bold move of confidence and authority, she tells the servants, "Do whatever He tells you!" I can just see her smiling back at Him as if responding to His challenge with an equal amount of daring love and adventure.

In her simple yet profound response, she not only declared that He *could* change things, but *would*. All that she had come to know through years of love and affection with this One she had borne, she knew His heart and pulled on it. This is what set things in motion for Jesus to turn the water into wine.

Without hesitation, Jesus told the servants to fill the water jars and take some to the master. There is no mention of debate. No indication of evaluating the consequences. There is only love responding to love. As a result, the master tastes this amazing wine and tells the bridegroom that this is not usual protocol! Where the best wine is usually served at the beginning, *this* wine was saved for the last! The Greek wording basically says, "This beautiful wine has been *watched over and guarded* for the last."

The whole point of this story is not a retelling of Jesus' first miracle. Turning water into wine was easy for Jesus. The real miracle was Mary's faith and bold declaration in knowing His heart and changing His mind.

We are in desperate need of new wine in the Church. We need a fresh infilling and empowering of the Spirit of God. Many have been waiting and watching, feeling like our wine is running out. We have questioned God, debating about when or how this outpouring of new wine will happen. Instead of pondering and debating eschatological signs and wonders, perhaps we should be responding like Mary did.

Perhaps it's time to step out in a bold faith that His love is stronger than our interpreting of the times.

Yes, there are things that need to align – just as prophesies needed to be fulfilled before the cross. But, have we so focused on religious checklists and prophetic fulfillment that we have forgotten the very essence and nature of His heart? For those who have been praying and waiting for God to reveal Himself, He is reminding us that the best is yet to come…if we but press in!

He is looking for some Mary's to respond to His voice and pull on His heart to break through the traditions of man and religious protocol to release the fresh wine of His Spirit.

Time may be in His hands, but the power to release the wine is in ours.

Lord Jesus, thank You for saving the best 'til last! Thank You for the promise of Your Spirit that is here now and still yet to be. I joyfully anticipate a greater move of Your Spirit upon the earth. I want to be like Mary who pulls on Your heart for more! Remind me to inquire of You and ask for a greater measure of Your presence, Your Spirit, and Your truth. I pray that I might be a vessel that pours out of the overflow in my own life to those around me. I pray that I would be filled with the new wine that is fresh and full of power. May You be glorified in this outpouring and may we tarry expectantly and with great hope for all that You have promised. In Jesus' name, amen!

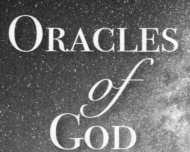

ORACLES *of* GOD

Words from the Father, Son, and Holy Spirit to the Church . . .

BE A CARRIER

"I have called you to not only carry a message, but to *be* the message. The power of My presence is best revealed through a vessel that carries it. You will become My Word as you are a carrier of My presence."

"There was one whom I called my friend who did this before you. I revealed Myself to Moses through the burning bush and he knew the power of My presence from the start. He knew the gravity of his call and knew he could not do it unless My presence went with him."

And he said to Him, "If Your presence will not go with me,
do not bring us up from here."
Exodus 33:15

"Out of his desperation and human frailties, he drew away to spend time in My presence and when he came down from that place My glory so covered him that people knew who I was."

When Moses came down from Mount Sinai ...
Moses did not know that the skin of his face shone
because he had been talking with God.
Exodus 34:29

"People need a burning bush encounter. Become my burning bush to call people into My manifest presence. Keep the fire burning in your own heart and let My glory flow from you just as it did from Moses when he came down the mountain. This message is a revelation of My heart and purposes. But, without it being carried by a vessel of My presence, it will bear no life and no fruit."

"There is the revelation and there is My presence. The revelation will open people's eyes, but it is My presence that will open people's hearts. Be the one who carries that."

"As I told my friend: My presence will go with you and I will give you rest."

CLOSE
THE BREACH

"There is a breach that has been opened over this nation. It is a breach in the Church that the enemy is coming through to steal, kill, and destroy the purposes of God. It is the divide between the Spirit and Word that has created a breach in the body of Christ."

"The Spirit and the Word must come together."

"The Spirit reveals the supernatural expression of the Father. He is One who cannot be understood and is beyond our comprehension, plans, or objective mindsets. He is forever moving and speaking, yet unchanging in purpose."

But when He, the Spirit of truth, comes, He will guide you into all the truth. He will not speak on His own; He will speak only what He hears, and He will tell you what is yet to come.
John 16:13

"The Word is eternal, foundational, and fully true and trustworthy. It is the Word that establishes the unchanging nature of God and it is both written and spoken."

In the beginning was the Word, and the Word was with God, and the Word was God.
John 1:1

"But, these two must come together. One cannot exist without the other. There is a tension between these two camps of the Church that has created a breach. Whereas they are to work together, the church has divided over these expressions of the Godhead. Doctrinal differences have separated Christ's Body. It is through this breach that the enemy has a foothold in the Church and in this nation."

"The breach must be filled! Stand in the gap and intercede for this breach to be filled. It is not about objective versus subjective truth. It is not about preferences or doctrines. It is about the fullness of Jesus being revealed."

"Jesus Christ is the center. He is the one Who stands in the gap to bridge the walls of division. He is the One Who has accomplished all at the cross and has been forever interceding for His Church, His Bride to be one, just as He and the Father are one. The Spirit and Word are expressions of Christ and He alone can make things one."

"Now is the time to stand in the gap and intercede. Do not criticize those you do not understand. Do not condemn those who are a different expression of the Godhead. Honor, esteem, and submit to one another out of reverence for Christ Who is in all, through it all, above it all, and the center of everything we do. Heaven is coming to manifest fully on the earth. But, the Spirit and Word must be one in order to receive its fullness."

"Die to self. It is only in the crucified life that you can withstand the pressure of the gap. It is only through the power of the Holy Spirit being lived out through dead men and women – those who have died to their own preferences and opinions of how things should take place."

"Stand in the gap! Close the breach! Jesus will work in you and through you, and bring all things together so that the Spirit and Word reveal the fullness of the Father and all He has planned from the foundation of time."

PREPARE THE WAY

"Prepare the way, believer. Prepare the way for Me to come." "Remove every roadblock and hindrance that would keep you distant from My presence. I tell you I am coming soon and I am holding back time to give you time to prepare."

"Satan has asked to sift you as wheat, but I have prayed that you would remain strong and courageous. The battles you see in the natural only mirror the eternal battle that rages for you. Be more concerned with the war for your soul than the wars between nations."

"I have already overcome the world, but I desire to overcome you."

"I long to come in My fullness but you must get ready. You must fix your eyes on Me and not get distracted. You must clear the clutter and compromise. You must pursue Me like never before. Time is short and My heart longs to see you face to face."

"Seek the low way for it is in the low place that you will find Me. There are many who seek Me in the public eye making their journey to Me a ministry rather than a mystery. I look for those who are small in the world's eyes but large in Mine. I delight in simplicity of faith and purity of heart that needs no validation from others. It is in the secret place that I reveal the secrets of My heart to those whose only goal is to pursue Me."

"There is no time left to build individual kingdoms. There is only one Kingdom and one goal. It is to reveal Me and My glory to a world that is dying."

"It must be done as One. One body, one Church, one Bride that does not seek reputation or the gaze of others' adoration. My kingdom will only be displayed through a Body that is united together on their faces in the place of rest and My presence."

"Do not look for Me on billboards or in social media. Do not look for Me in the crowds or arenas of popularity. Do not look for Me to market Myself to religion. Though My presence will invade every one of those areas, it will start in the secret place with you; one person, one soul, one who has given everything else away to seek Me."

"Who of you is willing to give up your personal ambitions and dreams in order to seek only Me? My kingdom will be established through one Bride, not individuals pursuing ministries. That time was, but is not now. Now is the time to join together as one expression, to become carriers and living demonstrations of My glory. Your gifts were given to glorify Me, not yourselves or your vision. I cannot share My glory with another. Use your gifts to serve one another and seek Me."

"Prepare the way. Prepare as one. I am looking. I am watching. I am waiting for you to prepare and get ready. Then I will come."

A Tsunami of Praise!

I hear the cry of heaven in this hour to rise up from your seated positions of tarrying and waiting. Rise up and give Him praise! For the enemy has tried to drown out the praises of God through murmuring and complaining - but the praises of God can drown him out! The distractions that have come to the earth realm to stifle heaven's praise cannot withstand the praises of a holy people who are desperate to praise! Can you hear Him call? The Lord says:

"There is a tsunami of praise that has been building on the distant shores of heaven that is coming to the earth. Can you hear it?"

"Just as the enemy has been crying foul and screaming in your ears, heaven has been birthing its own sound of praise and goodness. Can you hear its rumble?"

It can and will overcome the sound of the enemy's lies and accusations. These present conflicts will not be overturned through rebukes or binding, alone. They will be overcome through those with the Word of God on their lips and the praises of God in their mouths! It will be those who have determined to rise up from the place of weariness and defeat, to praise the Lord of Hosts, that will be given authority over the sound of the enemy. This wave of praise has the power to open up portals and gates!

The floods have lifted up, O Lord, the floods have lifted up their
voice; the floods lift up their roaring.
Mightier than the thunders of many waters, mightier than the
waves of the sea, the Lord on high is mighty!
Psalm 93:3-4

The sound of these mighty rushing waters is the worship and praise of the angelic host, and the creatures around the throne of God, who have been declaring the holiness of God for all eternity. As we join this heavenly wave of praise, the glory it carries will come crashing into our midst and bring heaven to earth.

Though this call is for every son and daughter of the King, it is God's daughters in this hour that carry a sound of praise able to shatter the spirit of accusation and despair. It is a company of women who have known great pain, but come through in victory, who carry this sound of praise that will utterly destroy and demolish the vitriol of hatred and enmity against man.

Rise up, daughters, and let your praises be heard! Release the sound of victory to drown out the Accuser of the brethren and the hordes of demonic voices he directs. As overcomers who have defeated disappointment and despair, rise up and declare His triumph on high!

Rise up Church, and let the tsunami of praise crash on these shores through your voice. Declare His goodness in the land of the living to usher in resurrection life and glory. Know that, once released, this tsunami will not stop, for it is sent from heaven.

I am the Lord your God, who stirs up the sea so
that its waves roar; the Lord of hosts is His name.
And I have put My words in your mouth and covered you in the
shadow of My hand, establishing the heavens and laying the
foundations of the earth, and saying to Zion, "You are my people."
Isaiah 51:15-16

Wanda Alger and her husband, Bobby, have ministered together for over 25 years. After serving in pastoral leadership in the central Shenandoah Valley for six years, they moved to Winchester, Virginia in 1998 where they planted Crossroads Community Church and continue to serve. They are a partner church with DOVE International.

Wanda is a recognized five-fold prophetic minister with DOVE USA and is a field correspondent and writer with Intercessors for America (ifapray.org). After years of leading worship and raising their three children, she now writes her own weekly blog in addition to contributing to numerous online publications such as The Elijah List, Charisma, Christian Post, and Spirit Fuel. She also teaches at Crossroads and speaks upon request at various gatherings.

Additional Resources

Follow Wanda's Blog
at www.wandaalger.me

Join the online following to receive weekly posts from Wanda.

- Prophetic words and insights
- Teaching articles
- Prayer resources
- Video clips

Provide your email and automatically receive new postings to your inbox so you can get ongoing fresh devotional thoughts to stir your spirit and grow your faith.

Prophetic Coaching Seminar DVD Set

This Prophetic Coaching Seminar series is for beginners, as well as those who are more seasoned in the prophetic. Anyone who ministers in the prophetic gifts needs to be healthy, vibrant, and accurate. If you want to grow in this gift, as well as teach others about this important ministry in the body of Christ, this series is for you.

Available at **www.wandaalger.me**
and **www.crossroadswinchester.com**
or by calling Crossroads Community Church at 540-722-4035

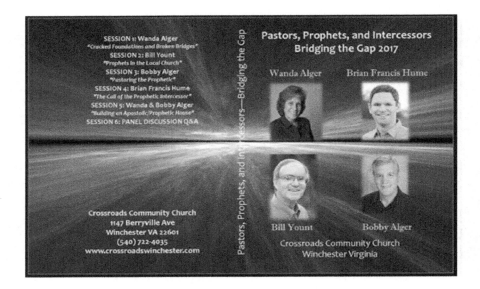

Pastors, Prophets, and Intercessors Conference DVD Set

Our prayers and proclamations have greater authority when we get rightly aligned, not only with heaven, but with one another. At a time when healthy apostolic/prophetic ministry is critical, these sessions will address common communication gaps and misunderstandings within the Church and bring clarity to the calls and functions of our gifts in this season. We must seek heaven for a greater oneness of His Spirit as we contend for revival in our nation and in our own back yards.

Available at **www.wandaalger.me**
and **www.crossroadswinchester.com**
or by calling Crossroads Community Church at 540-722-4035

Dream Interpretation
CD Series

Do you dream a lot and wonder what they mean? Do you wish you had more dreams and could learn how to interpret them? This series includes over 4 hours of teaching on dreams from a biblical perspective, including scriptural references for how to interpret, as well as many practical illustrations. God is speaking to you! Learn His language through the night parables He gives us.

Available at **www.wandaalger.me**
and **www.crossroadswinchester.com**
or by calling Crossroads Community Church at 540-722-4035

Making Room for His Presence:

21-Day Community Fast Devotional Guide

If we long for our communities to see the tangible presence of God permeate our cities and bring lasting transformation, we must prepare the way through personal consecration. The key essentials of humility, holiness, and unity must take root in our hearts personally before we can apprehend them corporately. This 21-Day Prayer Guide provides not only biblical admonitions and practical prayer points, but guides participants through an entire 21-Day experience as a community of believers that will make way for God's presence to come and dwell.

Sample preview of guide is available
at **www.wandaalger.me** and **www.crossroadswinchester.com**

Made in the USA
Monee, IL
02 February 2021